The Long White Thread of Words
Poems for John Berger

The Long White Thread of Words
Poems for John Berger

edited by Amarjit Chandan,
Gareth Evans and
Yasmin Gunaratnam

Smokestack Books
1 Lake Terrace, Grewelthorpe, Ripon HG4 3BU
e-mail: info@smokestack-books.co.uk
www.smokestack-books.co.uk

Cover image:
'White Roses offered by John to Melina'
copyright Yves Berger.

ISBN 978-0-9934547-4-5

Smokestack Books is
represented by Inpress Ltd

'...poems, even when narrative, do not resemble stories. All stories are about battles, of one kind or another, which end in victory or defeat. Everything moves towards the end, when the outcome will be known. Poems, regardless of any outcome, cross the battlefields, tending the wounded, listening to the wild monologues of the triumphant or the fearful. They bring a kind of peace. Not by anaesthesia or easy reassurance, but by recognition and the promise that what has been experienced cannot disappear as if it had never been. Yet the promise is not of a monument. (Who, still on a battlefield, wants monuments?) The promise is that language has acknowledged, has given shelter, to the experience which demanded, which cried out.'

John Berger
And Our Faces, My Heart, Brief as Photos

Words I

for Beverly

Down the gorge
        ran
            people and blood

In the bracken
        beyond touch
            a dog howled

A head between lips
        opened
            the mouth of the world

Her breasts
        like doves
            perch on her ribs

Her child sucks the long
        white thread
            of words to come

John Berger

Contents

Editors' Introduction   13
David Constantine, John Berger's Poetry   15

Alev Adil, *Milk the Moon*   21
Adonis, *You Are in the Village Then*   22
Anthony Anaxagorou, *Old Men from the Wall*   25
Joan Anim-Addo, *A Place of Visions*   26
Khairani Barokka, *Baffle Roof*   28
John Burnside, *The Visible*   29
Cevat Çapan, *Once in Europa*   31
Amarjit Chandan, *Mapping Memories*   32
Jeremy Clarke, *Music for Amen*   33
Francis Combes, *Spring Necklace*   39
David Constantine, *Ways of Being*   40
Andy Croft, *Massacre*   41
Mangalesh Dabral, *The Accompanist*   43
Claudia Daventry, *The Ikon-Maker's Son*   44
Richard Dehmel, *Deep from Far*   47
Kristin Dimitrova, *Three Old Masters*   48
Tishani Doshi, *The Leather of Love*   51
Rosalyn Driscoll, *Angel of History*   53
Sasha Dugdale, *Days*   54
Ian Duhig, *The White Page*   59
Tim Etchells, *to check the rain*   60
Gareth Evans, *In Secret*   61
Elaine Feinstein, *Muse*   69
John Fennelly, *Looking at Armenian Family Photographs*   70
S.J. Fowler, *The bear stands upon its hind legs*   72
Carolyn Forché, *The Lightkeeper*   73
Linda France, *Watching 'Norte, The End of History'*   74
Lavinia Greenlaw, *Louder but quieter*   76
Dan Gretton, *Plums in January, Pen Llŷn*   77
Jay Griffiths, *Encompassing*   79
Sam Guglani, *Fingerprints*   80
Yasmin Gunaratnam, *Words 0*   81
Golan Haji, *Autumn Here is Magical and Vast*   83

David Harsent, *Nuit Blanche* 85
Susan Hibberd, *an autumn's day* 86
Ellen Hinsey, *The Laws* 87
Graeme Hobbs, *Notes on Love* 89
Michael Hrebeniak, *Response to 'Here is Where We Meet'* 91
Nader Al-Hussein, *More Honour Than* 93
Kathleen Jamie, *Landfall* 94
Abdulkareem Kasid, *The Rat King* 95
Carlos Laforêt, *Still more marvellous* 96
Chris McCabe, *'seeing comes before words'* 97
Nikola Madzirov, *Home* 98
Valerio Magrelli, *Child Labour* 99
Caroline Maldonado, *On the eve of Ferragosto* 100
Bejan Matur, *Time Consoled in the Stone* 101
Sophie Mayer, *Goldene Yoykh* 103
Arvind Krishna Mehrotra, *My Mother's New Bras* 105
Anne Michaels, *To Write* 106
Gérard Mordillat, *What Are We Talking About?* 109
Andrew Motion, *The White Bear* 110
Daljit Nagra, *Naugaja* 112
Mukoma Wa Ngugi, *Portraits of my Grandfather* 115
Víctor Rodríguez Núñez, *three ways of seeing* 118
Sean O'Brien, *The Rain it Raineth* 121
Michael Ondaatje, *In official histories* 122
Ruth Padel, *The Wild One* 123
Mark Pajak, *Brood* 124
Mario Petrucci, *the dead   do not* 126
Claudia Rankine, *February 26, 2012* 128
Jeremy Reed, *On Stage* 130
Angus Reid, *94/365* 131
Robin Robertson, *Storm, Nissaki* 132
Mark Robinson, *Homewards* 133
Michael Rosen, *Who was a Communist?* 135
Fiona Sampson, *Cuckoo* 138
Clare Sandal, *I long to walk* 140
Jim Scully, *All That is Solid* 141
Iain Sinclair, *Stateless Passport* 143
Richard Skinner, *'Fabiola'* 144

Jura Soyfer, *Matuska Speaks*   145
Esta Spalding, *from 'Origins'*   146
Gerda Stevenson, *Syrian Artist*   148
Susan Stewart, *After the Mowing*   149
Arundhathi Subramaniam, *Tongue*   153
Paul Summers, *ligne rouge*   155
Michael Symmons Roberts, *Orison*   156
George Szirtes, *Photograph at a Table*   157
Raymond Tallis, *Decembrance*   159
Elisabete Tolaretxipi, *The Fish*   160
Thanasis Triaridis, *Seville, 21st century*   161
Wana Udobang, *Home*   163
Gilles Bernard Vachon, *For John Berger, Poet*   165
Pierre Vieuguet, *Step by Step*   166
Stephen Watts, from *Journey Across Breath*   167
Tamar Yoseloff, *Body Language*   170
zhu zhu, *blue smoke*   171
Rafeef Ziadah, *Passport*   174

Contributors   176
Acknowledgements   193

Editors' Introduction

As a writer who has worked in every possible form for seven decades, John Berger chooses to identify himself as a 'storyteller'. Whatever the framework, prompt or holding vessel, he has always sought out stories – of art and of being in the world – as the best way to capture the truths of lived experience, the impulse of resistance and the necessity of hope. Unlike modern capital, which brutally severs people from their pasts, present and futures with a constantly receding and ungraspable promise, stories offer individuals, communities and cultures a sensuous means to know, and change, their place in the world.

Perhaps surprisingly, one title Berger would not give himself is that of 'poet'. Poetry is an action for Berger, not a title. It is about doing (from its Greek etymology meaning 'to make'). It is an act of use. Because of that, he has of course 'smuggled' poems into many of his prose volumes. He clearly enjoys the possibilities afforded by the formal distinction, precision and rhythmic rigour of poetry and how poems are hospitable to mystery and non-linear temporalities.

It is also important to note that many of the writers closest to Berger's own heart – from Akhmatova to Tsvetaeva, Joszef to Pasolini, Césaire to Darwish and Hikmet to Ritsos, to name only a few – are writers of poetry. It was out of these two grounds, Berger's own poems and the influence of those writers he loves, that this anthology has grown[1].

The invitation to contribute a poem went out to writers we know and admire from across the world. They include globally recognised, award-winning authors, alongside established, emerging and outstanding younger names. In every case, their response was wholehearted and enthusiastic. They were delighted to gather together in words – for Berger 'the only human home, the dwelling place' – and take part in this collec-

---

[1] The South African writer and activist Richard Pithouse has recently provided a superb commentary on both of these aspects of Berger in *The Con* magazine; see theconmag.co.za/2015/02/23/the-living-voice/

tive act of celebration and gratitude. The majority of the poems here have been written specially for this volume. Where that was not possible, previously published pieces were carefully identified and chosen. This is a truly international collection. There are poems from African, Chinese, Indian, Iraqi, Kurdish, Palestinian, and Syrian poets, as well as those living in exile, reflecting the global reach and resonance of Berger's writing. The poems range from the intimate to the social, from the experimental to the testimonial, and all, in their unique way, express and honour the importance of John Berger's extraordinary work to this wonderfully gifted comradeship of makers.

We are delighted that this collection is being published by the radical poetry press Smokestack Books, and thank publisher Andy Croft for his faith in the project from the outset. It is of course the ideal home for such a volume. Smokestack has always committed itself proudly to its regional base in England's North East while maintaining a strikingly internationalist perspective within its list. Smokestack's publication of Berger's own collected poems in 2014 (following the 1994 first gathering of Berger's verse in *Pages of the Wound*) confirms the regard in which the press is held by the writer that these pages celebrate.

The Long White Thread of Words was initiated by Amarjit to celebrate Berger's 90th birthday, but its relevance, worth and beauty stand outside of any specific anniversary. We can think of no other writer who commands such passionate respect, and from such a fecundity of voices. In refusing to separate the evidence of the work from the example of his life, John Berger has changed the course of many lives and has enriched all who have read and known him. It is a privilege to be able to offer him this collective gift in thanks for all he has given us, and we are grateful to every writer and to John's son Yves, who made such a gift possible and supported us throughout.

Onwards!

AC, GE, YG
October 2016

John Berger's Poetry

'He was a poet and hated approximations.'
Rilke, *The Notebooks of Malte Laurids Brigge*

Moving to Quincy, Haute-Savoie, in 1973, John Berger deliberately put himself among realities he had no close knowledge of; and as writer, villager and worker learned about them thereafter.

The *Gestus* of John Berger's *Collected Poems* (Smokestack Books, 2014) is that of a man looking. He is looking closely at the world around him, at people in it, at how they live among the facts of their lives – and how they might live, better or worse, when those facts alter. Then in the writing of the poem, the *Gestus* is much the same: a man concentrating, looking into himself for the words to say what he has seen and listening closely for the sound and rhythms of those words line by line as the poem grows. These poems are careful, their author wishes to be as exact as possible.

The arrangement of the book is thematic: Words, History, Emigration, Places, My Love. So it happens that poems decades apart in chronology are collected together, or may even face one another, in their topics. Easy to see then how careful he always was, how he has always hated approximations. 'Leavings', a poem of 1956/7, refers to itself, its own way of proceeding, as 'these cautious lines'. 'Alpage' proceeds, in that sense cautiously, through seven precise instances, ordered like seven haikus: 'Murmuring river/ clasps the mist/ for a moment more'. 'Distant Village' works similarly, through ten compact triplets.

Berger's whole oeuvre – poetry, fiction, political and literary essays – is of a piece. Some poems in this volume are taken from, among other books, *Pig Earth* and *Once in Europa*. They appear there not as lyrical interludes but as further condensations of accounts, events, characters, in the prose. Re-reading *Pig Earth*, I saw again and again how apt to become poetry – *his* own poetry – his prose is. 'Ladle' and 'Ladder', for example, out of the closest observation of the thing itself extend (and intensify!) into a realization of that object as one made and used by human beings and steeped in their lives in their locality. The ladle is of pewter, pock-marked and moon-shaped. The poem celebrating it finishes:

> Ladle
> pour the sky steaming
> with the carrot sun
> the stars of salt
> and the grease of the pig earth
> pour the sky steaming
> ladle
> pour soup for our days
> pour sleep for the night
> pour years for my children

The poem 'The Unsaid' has as its subject 'a pile of letters/not yet replied to', among which, Berger writes, are some 'from poets/ more lyrical than I/requesting advice…' Enigmatic lines! Do such poets wish to be more like him? Or do they make him wonder should he be more like them?

It is not *despite* their thorough political engagement that Aimé Césaire and Mahmoud Darwish are great lyric poets, and Berger's translations of them (with Anna Bostock for the first and Rema Hammami for the second) are proof of a lyrical abilty which, perhaps, he has deliberately restrained in poems of his own. Poetry has many ways to the truth. Berger has shaped his for his life's work, worked at it for a coherent purpose.

Trying to see exactly, trying to learn, and set down for others to learn, the truth, is of itself, in times as mendacious as ours, an act of humane revolt.

The book's sections are, of course, porous, but their order is significant. Words first. History then is the stuff of the poems made of words and is itself the context of Emigration, Places and My Love. The words, as poems, are always an act *in* that context and very often, one way or another, they are an act *against* it. 'They Are the Last' is an elegy for the animals ('Each year more animals depart…. Now that they have gone/ it is their endurance we miss'). The poem is addressed to Berger's late wife Beverly, in their village. But in the lament an objection is recorded. The elegy is itself a revolt. Berger quotes Mr L. J. Taylor, of the Wall's Meat Company: 'The breeding sow …/should be thought of and treated/as a valuable piece of machinery/whose function/ is to pump out baby pigs'. That mindset, that way of being in and dealing with the world, won't be halted by Berger's poem. But saying no to overwhelming forces is evidence of a presently being defeated but perhaps one day recoverable human and more humane possibility. So, poets, object! Such an objection exceeds the poet and the like-minded person to whom this poem is addressed. The reach of a poem is incalculable. Starting in a particularity and addressed to a particular person, it generalizes, so that, here, our whole relationship with our fellow-creatures is implicated, and reaching its readership, which may one day be millions, it will encourage the like-minded in their struggle and, who knows, may unsettle the unlike-minded in their opinions.

As Brecht did, John Berger understands himself as 'exemplary' of the times he is living through. 'Self-portrait 1914-18', in the History sequence, opens:

> It seems now that I was so near to that war.
> I was born eight years after it ended
> When the General Strike had been defeated.
>
> Yet I was born by Very Light and shrapnel
> On duck boards
> Among limbs without bodies.

That is, he feels himself to be stained 'like the dyer's hand' by that first colossal mechanized slaughter (and, certainly, by all the atrocity since). See also in that section 'Born 5/11/26' – or 'Orlando Letelier, 1932-1976', which again is both elegy and denunciation. Letelier, one of Allende's ministers, living in exile in Washington DC, was murdered there on General Pinochet's orders (documents released by President Obama in 2015 prove it).

Poets set their own constellations in the night sky. 'Robert Jorat' is an elegy for a friend and teacher. It opens:

> This morning Robert
> I polished my black boots
> to be correct and neat
> for your adieu

Continues:

> You taught me
> the dying art
> of sharpening a scythe
> with a hammer

And ends:

> Next June
> I must sharpen the scythe alone
> and for you I will try Robert
> to make it sharper than my grief

Dead friend, dying art – and the poem: saying, saying, saying.

David Constantine

Milk the Moon

Did your father milk the moon
just for you
pour luminous liquid
poison in a cold stone cup?

Did your mother sew
a tiny sparrow
into your breast
beating against your bones?

What did you inherit?
Did they tell you everything
you could see
just as you closed your eyes?

How many languages do you speak?
Can you speak the breeze in the mountains,
a smattering of summer rain,
of the silence just before the dawn?

Tell me now lover
while I'm listening
unlace your courage
leave it folded on the chair.

We're hungry for life
like wolves
we're not done
crying for the moon.

Alev Adil

You Are in the Village Then

1

When he leaves home carrying his axe, he is certain that the sun is waiting for him in the shade of an olive tree, or a willow, and that the moon that crosses the sky tonight over his house will take the road closest to his steps. It is not important to him where the wind goes.

2

The blueness of the sky, the redness of fruit, the greenness of leaves: These are the colours that his hands spread on the page of day.

He is an artist who cares about his hands' work, not what the hands of art achieve, but the things inside things, and not as they appear, but how he describes them. And because he knows how to listen to things and how to speak to them, he lives on the margin of what people perceive. He believes that 'the order that imprisons motion and interrupts the feasts of the imagination will only lead to collapse.'

And it collapses without theatrics or noise. He knows 'that a bullet now replaces his plough,' but he also knows, with growing certainty, that 'his plough will go further and that it will reach deeper than any bullet can.'

3

When you see this farmer carrying his plough, you sense then that he is competing with it as if in a war. It proceeds ahead of him toward the weeds and thorns and he remains barefoot, following behind. The sound of the plough, as it tears at the thorns and soil, joins you, penetrates you, and it's lovely to hear it become loud like a trumpet with a deep raspy blow filling the sky.

4

You are in the countryside then. It does not matter where you walk now, near the river or at the foot of a mountain, or a village lost among the rocks, where mud houses mix with cement cellars in a folkloric symphony that combines the tenth and the twentieth centuries. Let your eyes swim in all that's around them, forget the café and the street. Surrender like a leaf flying in the air, like the fuzz coating the branches, like pollen dust. Become a child. Only then will invisible creatures come toward you. Solitude filled with a treasure of hidden murmurs. Absence that instantly becomes a presence. Each tree is a person, each stone a sign.

There are herds of small animals that shine like distant stars, among grasses and plants. And there are stones that have heads and arms and that may walk behind you at night. There are small streams flitting among small trees that become beautiful maidens who appear to tired people heading to their houses before dawn, during the first hours of enchantment.

5

The village is not a poet, as much as it is a painter. There is a remarkable ease to its touch as it draws the same picture every single day maintaining the same beauty. It is repetition that does not repeat the same motion, something like the waves of the sea, or like the desert renewed endlessly in sand, its only dress. There is no uniqueness to this touch as if it comes from an absolute neutrality forever positioned at degree zero.

6

You are in the village then?

I remember now what I almost forgot. To contradict the light in the village, one will end up choosing solitude, sitting on the other side of the mountain, or the square, or among the barefoot children and black goats.

And I remember now that we used to gaze at the stream covered with green grasses, hardly able to determine its course. We thought it was in pain, and moaning.

And I now know why we felt dried up in the memory of the stream.
And in the days now inscribed in the dust of the road leading to the stream, I also read what we knew and did not know to write: Peace to the sun that always went ahead of us, without ever moving.

Adonis
Translated by *Khaled Mattawa*

Old Men from the Wall

A third winter sets on brick walls
chipped with a luck that looks like bone.
I walk a lot these days, noting the old men
who never leave their spot. They huddle
around one another from morning
until the junk grass grows brave enough
to take off its thick white pelt
and the estate can again go back
to being an expired advent calendar
the children long ago renounced.

But for the men, where are their wives?
Who waits to hear their stories?
They pack no clues inside the slits of their coats.
Nails stubbed down to the grime, opening tin
with pebble teeth. Blood cuts their faces
like a volley of whispers too loud to lose
again, ammonia leaks from the walls,
from the mouth of the alley where the trees
stream piss, piss leaking from the heavens,
yellow and rancid and holy stinging rain.

Legions of silver breath-cloud crashing chat
of lost bets and fights in their little dark;
there's the swindler Clive who disappeared
last week because he owed money
to some mug from over there or Johnny
who tried dying and seemed to like it.
I want to suggest something but I don't,
relics of the dirty road, nothing Gods
picking splinters from out their hearts
never hurting anyone but themselves.

Anthony Anaxagorou

A Place of Visions

Once, journeying over placid mountains
to a place where vehicles must stop
for the road narrowing to a small path,

the driver, speaking a tongue I did not know,
halted. He spoke to a man I did not know.
Nodding, he removed my case

from the car's trunk,
pointed to a snake's tail
of a path, slithering out of sight,

its scales camouflaged cobblestones
bearing centuries of dust.
And so I dragged my luggage

on roller wheels screaming over rock
cut at the outer edge for men's feet.
Below, green water stole the little breath

left from pulling upwards heavy belongings,
holding fraught nerves in check, and worrying
at the bend's sightline disappearing.

A small wooden boat waited
on green waters below
as if for painter and palette.

I wondered about the ferryman
who could not be seen. Nor was I ready.
(Another time I might have promptly paid).

The path offered a left fork to a bridge
across a chasm. A gate blocked the entrance
so that the bridge was locked tight

and when I stopped to let
the sudden breeze cool my temples
I gazed down again at the water

wondering anew that
it had travelled so high –
a foolish thought;

the water's travels had barely begun –
I was the climber beginning to sense folly;
the greater being to attempt a return.

Pressing forward around blind curves,
what relief when the path at last
opened to a wide cobbled yard

and a tiny house built from rock.
No-one. Though soon a mighty wind swirled
leaves– yellow and brown and small –

to beat mercilessly about my head.
Who knew of my coming, I wondered then
and why had a hurricane been sent to meet me?

Joan Anim-Addo

Baffle Roof

The structure above the boy napping
On a frame, hammocked by cerulean
Thread, wound round serpentine
And tied to its edges is a roof.

The pastels used to coat windowed
Barriers against the chill of Rajasthan's
November – another strain of roof.

The warm welcome of a woman,
Thirty-two, into the folds of the
Family she'd left for a husband
Who, like the others, piles bricks
In Qatar and accidentally sends
Her a picture of a woman with too
Much kohl round dark eyes, allowing
Her, finally, to kiss the man behind
The counter at the jewelry shop –
In broad daylight – causing consternation,
But somehow, reprieve; and in lieu of
Tears, this unexpected returning to,
Enveloping in, a deeper kind of love.

This, too, a roof.

Khairani Barokka

The Visible

Then it could be said: The visible exists
because it has already been seen.
John Berger

Winter felt dark this year.
No colder than usual, and never as dark as the night
when you and I stood in the garden,
pointing out the stars we knew by name;

but dark, when we sat in the kitchen to hear the news,
dark on the drive to work, and still darker at noon,
or at dusk, when I brought in the logs and nobody spoke,
the garden as far from our thoughts

as Cassiopeia.
Now, on the cusp of spring, there are days when we feel
like the people in Hitchcock films,
the lovely quotidian frayed at the edge to reveal

a story we always feared would catch us out,
not, when we think of it, wishing for stories at all,
only the sweet familiar, the flowering cherries
finding their way to rose-pink and almost-crimson,

after the brief distraction of the snow,
the tidy arrangement of sunlight between the houses,
stair-rails and street trees
edged with the usual gold.

So could it be this we intend
when we speak of fate,
that everything we know was seen before,
though not by us?

how so much of the starlight we have named
is drifting away,
like the snowlines that melted for days
in the neuks of the trees,

or the carol that stayed in my head and would not budge
all the way home in the dark, till the turn of the year,
a sense of impending grace in the not-yet-seen,
a part-song, in common time, that refused to be gone.

John Burnside

Once in Europa

for John Berger

When evening settles on the mountain slopes,
if you hear a knock at your door, it's us –
like the sounds of flute and lute
in the old summerhouses of İçerenköy
in a time that is past and present and to come,
in summer nights fresh with the scent of pine:
two sleepwalkers never to be parted,
wandering, calling at lost addresses.

Last time we saw you, you were in a film:
Play Me Something. On a Scottish island
you were telling a story set in Mestre
to passengers waiting for a plane.
It's time to make hay, you write –
a writer in winter and a labourer in summer!
They are rich with it too, your books,
with the scent of cut grass and tilled soil:
Pig Earth, Once in Europa,
and now *Lilac and Flag.*

In spring,
  when the snow is gone from the mountain slopes,
  if there is an unexpected knock at your door.
  it's us –
          the seventh man,
                            the seventh woman,
with lilacs and flags.

Cevat Çapan
Translated with *Michael Hulse*

Mapping Memories

Imagine it is a paper.
Look at it.
It is a portrait of the earth.
See where the needle of your magnetic heart stops.
That's it. That's the place you always missed.

Put a dot.
Touch it with your fingertip. Softly.
It throbs.
Then put another, and then another till a line is formed –
The umbilical cord reconnecting.

The spot is the cartograph of your memories.
It is the wound healed.

A dot shines on the page
    at the zero degree of all directions.
Here ends your returning.
You are home.

Amarjit Chandan

Music for Amen

I   The sun hunting into daylight
choir: a place is lit by our love for it

I was here before the wind. Before the sun coloured in.
    Cars are necklace beads
being strung on a distant string.
    It will take forever.

I watch a city grow on one horizon,
    standing asleep
in its own noise. There will be birdsong, and light arriving
    in a slow surprise.

II   A winter tree is defined by the sky
choir: shadow is one interpretation of the light

The long ground knows where I am, what I've been doing.
    It follows me everywhere.
Green uneven miles scored by lines of road. A wind
    let loose in it

to learn it all. Green is the ground's first thought,
    one dream of its sleep.
In the early air my breath. On the ground the grass
    correcting itself in my wake.

III   In the sliding hours the struck stone sings
choir: a season's moment of animation

The arriving light touches one thing at a time. It's naming
   everything. Nothing
is out of place. A day's orange ends, the copper shadows.
   A group of trees are dividing

the light amongst themselves. I keep going
   until I find the spot. Sky
is everywhere. The mind forgets its thousand things.
   Blue is the colour of faraway.

IV   Between the two immensities of light and dark
choir: our holding and holding back

I mark out the space. The sun makes a start on the city's glass.
   Winter light never quite
comes to ground, never grabs hold of anything.
   The wind burns. The body, all

restlessness and belonging, bends to its task. There are
   moments of music, broken
by birdsong. I tear the wind, I carry the ground, all day long
   trains underline the horizon.

V   What is familiar is indescribable
choir: the face of the wind in its sleep

In the far-off city a church clock chimes. Each note drops into the air
    like an item on a list. Every sound
is a flash of something opening, something being lost. The struck
    hours move. A blade of grass can tell

the difference between raindrop and dewfall the way
    a tree leaf knows a light wind's
six kinds of slightly. A single repeated movement, the plainsong
    of something done by rote.

VI   The visible waits to be seen
choir: the colour of laughter is yellow

Trees are measuring the distance between blue and green.
    All the men that I am
is one small effort against the effortless. In the bowl of the spade
    the woken ground's

first lessons in air. It dries, begins to lighten, falls apart. A white stone
    knows the light will come. Blind
light thinks white a window. At my back the city is one
    struck match after another.

VII   We walk in the dark until it becomes the light
choir: a heart stops where it belongs

Ground is a single thing and can't be separated from itself
    or taken away. I'm making a pile of it
on top of it. Breath against breath. The wind is something gone
    too far, is miles

of complicated sleep, like ground, one sense, all feeling,
    like light, a heart
isn't in it. Ground under ground, the size of the quiet when I stop
    for a moment.

VIII   A blown leaf is a refugee from purpose
choir: wide rain walks the earth in songs

No colour in this country, for the alarmed eye scouring the space
    no sanctuary of difference. Brown
after brown and the dulled ear's hope of a stone
    in the spade's catchphrase.

The senses are the first to grieve, yearn for an imagined bliss.
    Hurrying heart, this
is what it is to rest. The wind blowing over, light pulling itself away,
    slow dark breaking into darks.

IX   Tricks of the light in the hovering instant
choir: to look and not look away

In penniless winter the light soon spends an afternoon.
   I am practising simplicity,
the calm I will be. Sky is a lesson in extravagance and restraint,
   in never being surprised

or asleep. The long light sharpens its shadows, advances
   its armies of absence. Each
spade of ground is a sample of surrender, every passing car a wind
   with a song in it.

X   The sun can find a field's gold
choir: the blue at the back of the world

A blackbird singing, an evening delicate and naive. Cold sun
   setting everything alight,
taking everything with it. It will always be winter, a loose wind
   loving what we can't.

The slim city watching, coming on. Every thing is attached
   to the light. I will be white
in my room. A single silence in a hidden country. One slip of the
   sun and it's gone.

XI   Like something standing at the end of summer
choir: church bells silver the air

Dusk is a child's dark, a night on its knees, introducing itself.
    The light says forget
not yet. This is no slow hand over. The light will continue
    as the dark. Radiant earth

in light's late reds, light coming clear. Tender deep
    I have lifted, every ounce
I have made my own. It will come back to me, the folded heart
    held like a stone.

XII   The wind has no word for rest
choir: a river carries itself away

Helplessly the night comes, making a space of everything, huge
    and waiting, wide open.
The sky has pulled back. There is nothing and no end to it. I am
    almost out of sight. I can see

my breath, the faraway movement of me. My eye holds to the light
    of passsing cars, a train's lit
room after room. The city is shining. The dark insists,
    insists.

Jeremy Clarke

Spring's Necklace

The mountain is there very near
like a great closed leather bag,
an abandoned sack of treasure
heavy with stones, with fatigues, with secrets.

We are sitting outside
around the big wooden table
and we talk in the sunshine.

As we talk of poetry, revolution, the world,
John's grand-daughter
plucks from the grass the heads of dandelions
then, with all the seriousness children are capable of
when they play,
she comes and puts them down, in a row,
in the grooves of the table to decorate it
like a necklace
little insolent battalion of sunshine
defying the winter in our hearts

Spring in a child's hand
enough
never to despair of beauty.

Francis Combes
Translated by *Alan Dent*

Ways of Being

When let, when annoying nobody's neighbour
How thoroughly and all in their own good time
They become what they had it in them to become
In the small buried talent. I saw one a week ago
It had ascended like smoke on a windstill day

Slender, the tip of it feeling at the air
As delicately as an elephant's trunk. Walt Whitman
Thought he could turn and live with the animals
Who would not blather at him about his duty to God
And the chain-saw man next door. Myself

I'll seek acceptation among the trees. They do not
Run around all over the place snarling and bellowing
But stay still, moving in the fresh air. Another
I met that day, it reached out level and equally
On every side, in summer it would give you

A murmuring shade and the sight of yourself
Deep among the roots in a well shaft. It was of the kind
That cast themselves so abundantly over the earth
Scores of tractors and trailers lumbering down
Hard-rutted tracks from out of the deep province

Will mound a whole square high with colossal sacks
Of their light dry fragrance. The twinned helix
Is beautiful but for the naked eye the act itself appears
In ramification. You know by the bloodways
On your own shut lids how thirsty life is underground.

David Constantine

Massacre

after André Fougeron's Massacre de Sakiet III

How well we know these careless faces –
The children smiling in their sleep,
The ecstasy of death's embraces,
The naked girl thrown on a heap
Of awkward limbs and broken bodies.
The trophied heads. The silent squaddies.
We were not there the day the skies
Fell in, and yet we recognise
These peaceful and civilian features
So well we barely catch our breath;
Who are so intimate with death
We know these killings barely reach us;
But most of all we know whose boots
Stand guarding over empire's fruits.

Such knowledge must be classified
So you and I can sleep at night,
And five-year olds, once pacified
By bombs, must be hushed out of sight
By spokesmen with imperial smiles.
How well we know their smooth denials
And how they help us understand
That deaths like these are never planned.
But air-strikes cost the tax-payer millions,
And if our aims are imprecise,
Then somebody must pay the price:
This shrouded crowd of dead civilians
Who look at us as if to say
They will not let us look away.

Since these were murdered in Tunisia
Collateral damage is the norm.
Since '58 Death's gotten busier;
From Shock and Awe to Desert Storm
Our wars are won by air-offensive;
In PR terms it's less expensive –
More bangs for bucks, more flesh per pound –
Than putting boots in on the ground.
And so the dead are always nameless,
Uncounted, slaughtered in a war
By enemies they never saw,
And we, whose dreams are always blameless,
Lie listening for the noiseless drone
Of desert whirlwinds we have sown.

Andy Croft

The Accompanist

Supporting the heavy monolith of the main singer's voice
His own was graceful, thin and quavering.
He is the singer's younger brother
Or a pupil
Or a distant relative who comes on foot to learn.
Since long ago
The resonance of his voice has echoed
The sonority of his master's;
And when the singer's lost his way
In the tangled jungle of melodic uplands
Or strays into the void of unstruck sound
Beyond the further reaches of the scale
It's the accompanist who holds the steady theme,
Gathering up the things the singer left behind,
Reminding him of childhood days
When he was a novice

When the singer's voice gives way in the higher register,
Inspiration deserting him and fervour waning,
An ashiness shedding from his voice
Then the accompanist's tones emerge to blend with his;
Or it may be that he joins in simply
To show the singer that he's not alone
And that the song that's sung and done
Can be sung anew once more
And that the audible faltering in his voice
Or his willful avoidance of the higher notes
Is evidence not of ineffectuality
But of humanity.

Mangalesh Dabral
Translated by *Rupert Snell*

The Ikon-Maker's Son

Once there was a peasant boy whose father
painted ikons in exchange for bread
who, dying, tried to teach his son his trade.
'But – why would I,' the young boy said

'when this outdated artefact you've made
has taken weeks, and I could just
sell airbrushed shots of famous men instead?'

'Take up the board,' his father said, 'you'll feel
its pulse in the heat of your hands. It yearns
beneath its white bologna chalk and china clay.
Look – both are bound with glue.
If you can feel this, son, you'll know
how you can make the sweet earth sing for you.'

'I'm sorry, Dad, that sounds a lot like crap,'
said our protagonist, who wasn't known
for sensitivity, but had the knack
of business and, as some girls said, was good in bed.

'I take this red clay bole, or yellow clay, more glue
boiled down from bones. I blend with foam
raised from the white of a hen's egg, drop
with honey, brush it on the empty gesso,
warmed without a ripple, on the sheer base – look',
his father, propped against his pillows, tried again. He didn't look,

being more concerned with slicking down his hair,
'and last, I blot the board with chamois.
Skin and bone, an egg, the earth that made us.
Breathe on fire to quicken the long-dead,
then we add gold leaf.'

'How much did that stuff cost?' his son broke in,
annoyed. His father shook his head.,

'Now gild it – letter-close
to *guilt* that we were born with – '
'*you* were maybe born with. *We* don't have no guilt,'
his first and lastborn said, 'now, where's my keys?
I want to take Jemima out to Annabel's.'

'I coax out light five centuries old,' his Dad went on,
regardless, 'slow, through layers of varnished water,
 floating up as though in ether. Look at this. It's beautiful.'

'Blimey,' said the boy, 'that looks a lot of bother, for a one-off.
Better if you made a mousepad out of that,
or print it on a mug. Or even make a transfer,
stick it on a bicycle and – geddit? – call it Bike-on.
That could work, and maybe make a buck.'

'Next to the ikon's glow,' his ailing father said,
'true flesh is drab, dark olive, almost black.
Silver hairlines to the eyes, the mouth,
make mortals less when icons stay the same.'

'The point is, in an age of time as money,
all this takes too long,' the boy says
as he sashays through the door and leaves us
in a fug of hip cologne,

and, as he drives off in his white saloon
to Annabel's
the quiet decades take his father's soul
and turn the ikon-maker into paint,

define his cheekbones, temples, bridge of nose,
the jawline, philtrum, black his brows, his eyelids,
pupil. Trace a line of faintest white around
the nimbus, just beneath the bevelled, blood-red

edge that holds his halo – for he has one,
now – a ring of 'glory': word that just means
fame, ambition, praise, renown, the things
in life he never chased or chose. So *glory*

be to gods whose images are code for us,
to us, inventors of the gods, for everything
made beautiful that's made in all our names,
to burnishing plain earth with flecks of gold.

Claudia Daventry

Deep from Far

From the evening's white surges
rises a star;
deep from far
the new moon emerges.

Deep from far,
from the dawn's grey surges,
the great pale bow reaches
for the star.

Richard Dehmel (1863-1920)
Translated by *Wolfgang Görtschacher* and *David Malcolm*

Three Old Masters

I   Christ and Saint Mary on Golgotha
           Hans Holbein the Elder (1460-1524)

They are standing close to each other
but with a gap between them
that will broaden.

She looks at him, crying for him.
He looks ahead,
crying for himself.

He sits on the cross which
so far lies on the ground.
So far.

She is all clothed, even her hair
hidden.
He is not any more.

His hands are bound in front.
His body will soon be
rendered meaningless.

The skulls of past people
are scattered about,
the sky is deep blue

for those coming after.
The painting is small and
difficult to notice.

II   The Massacre of the Innocents
      Master from Frankfurt (1460-1533?)

In the foreground a soldier,
in an exquisite silver-grey tonality,
stern but conscientious,
pierces his sword through
the tiny neck of an infant.
Looks like a geography teacher pressing
his pointer stick in some narrow isthmus
to embed it in memory.
The mother will hardly
forget the lesson.
In the background two women
have caught hold of his colleague:
one grips his hands to constrain him,
the other, clutching his throat, has raised
a clog over his head
to finish him off.
Good for you, girls.
Master from Frankfurt,
who are you, actually?

III   A Group Of Crucifixes
       Michel Erhart (1440/45- after 1522)

They are wooden. Naive. Scrupulously
polished and painted in human colour.
Jesus soars between the thieves
but looking none the better for it.

The three faces are twisted
into demure grimaces of horror.
The eye falls on the relatively slim
yet unathletic bodies and down below

rests on the feet.
The shins of the thieves,
in full accordance with the Gospel,
are broken,

but what a good job
they did –
the skin is torn open,
the bones sticking out.

The feet are twisted and tied
at an unnatural angle, and you almost
expect to see between knee and ankle
an extra joint.

Fifteenth century. Nobody noticed the faces.
In everything else they were experts.

Kristin Dimitrova

The Leather of Love

after John Berger

This morning I take the weathered
secateurs to stems of lantana as
a woman sometimes must. At the gate
a bee-eater suns himself and posts
a kiss to the breeze sidling on by.
Me in batik house-wrap from a departures
lounge. Bird in feathers. The strange and
marbled green of our kingdom. *Embrace the*
day, bird, I whisper. Just then white
clouds pass by, devastated as ghosts.
Bird and I look upwards. The sky's the size of
a wrinkle – winnowing and closing, the
way an absence will. Birdie's gone –
disappeared – who knows where, wrapped
in the morning's foreboding. Dragonflies in
drag, a water pump muffled by tarpaulins,
the sand and salt and shrub – this is what we
live with. And when we lie in bed and talk
of the body's failings, of the petulant dead, of
disenchantment and insufficient passion,
we're chewing through fears so thick our
teeth are beginning to rust. Passion's
how a poem's meant to breathe – the
air sacs funneling life into saline
lungs. *Come back!* I won't be like that woman in
the rhyme who swallows a bird, which
isn't to say you aren't delectable. You, who hides
in the foliage. Yoo hoo! You, who are
the czar of colour. The morning's hung
itself on a granite obelisk, waiting for you to
reappear. I pour light through my hands to make
brass, a bell, something to lure you from
your hiding place. I, who thought a

poem could be about a garden, a staple or hinge
on which another poem could be built. I, of
limited imagination. I offer you my skin,
which is the same as offering you the
universe that breathes wild, through leather,
that sews our stomachs to gunny bags of
love. Always and only is a poem about love.

Tishani Doshi

Angel of History

He hasn't much time.
Climbs into the boat he's built,
draws a pair of oars,
lowers them into black water,
pulls into night.
Exile. Forget. Echo.
He strains to hear meanings too low
for the ear. Slides through debris
backward, wings
pinioned by the wind.
Howling. Hinge. Turn.
His words burn the air,
falling among the fallen
ahead of him.

Rosalyn Driscoll

Days

*On Svetlana Aleksievich's book about women's experiences
in WWII,* War Doesn't have a Female Face

I

When all is said and done, the worst that has happened
Is only this: crawling in a ditch, naked, except for an old dress
Ripped throat to groin and stained with blood.
What, is this the worst the fates can cut out
For me with their long shears? I am not ashes
I have my wits. I have the shadows of memories
Grand pianos, cinemas, milk bluing in a storm
A man losing his child to a king who rode him down
Silently, on a road like this: long and unmetalled
With the waymarkers snapped at their hilts
The milestones toppled and disfigured.
I had a future, and remember it well,
How it was always there, like the promise of light
At the edges of the curtain.

II

It was only the nurses who made us feel shame
If they had come to know of it
They would have made us feel ashamed
We did not want them to know about it
We knew they would make us ashamed
If they had come to know about it
Only the nurses could do that

III

On Thursday I drove out of the city.
The land was old and barely alive
It gave me the geometric shock
When life unroots itself
And the rearview mirror shows
A woman on the horizon of a hole
Living, but incinerated.

She spoke, and it was not for a while
I knew it was me speaking.
She was practising what to do
If someone has a stroke,
If someone has a memory loss
Or his heart stops beating

IV

War is liquid-thought-fire
It burns the mind –
I feel you are burnt irretrievably
Your imagination exposes beams
Your memories are shapeless ruins.

I've been scalded. As when I pick the pan up wrong
Or let the steam hiss out over my hands.

I heard of men in steamboats
When the boiler blows
Tripe-men, who stand a few minutes
Whole but boiled.

V

The interpreter shows me a dusty parlour
And hands me a broom.
No one is as tidy as me, I pant
I get every little mote of dust into the pan
I use spit instead of water
This place will fucking shine.

But the dust falls and falls
Because every action
Has an equal and opposite
And my skin is wearing through
Shedding particles
Like white soot
On the mantelpiece.

VI

I could so easily give up my house
I've made a list of what to take:
Notebooks, phone and plug, handcream
A thermos, knife, warm clothes.
But it makes me anxious
That I will start to smell after twenty-four hours.

VII

My daughter does my hair in two pigtails
I like her holding it and twisting it up
I remember someone else putting it up
When I was a child.
I remember how she brushed it.
Me, in a hospital bed with a beaker.
I remember how she combed it
Carefully. Me in the parlour
With the candles lighting my way.

VIII

I have no right to grief
I am whole
I have no right to grief
I am whole
I have no right to grief
I am whole

IX

My wife was a stenographer
She typed the word rape
Forty times in one hour
She sat in a bank of women
Making records of what had been done
And she felt herself to be lucky
To be alive and unscathed.
My wife lost only a few near relatives
And a first husband
And she had a stillbirth
Whose name she wrote in water.

X

Their flag was a tablecloth from a basement
With marks where they stubbed out their cigarettes
And soup stains and rings where they set their glasses.
Not everyone died fighting.
Some, like my own
Died when he fell into a river.
He was drunk. He'd come looking for a coin

We never gave him one.
He said bitches.
He left staggering.

XI

A computer, a glass of wine.
A group of girls filmed in headscarves
By an enemy combatant.
You should hate me, he says,
I could kill your menfolk, your boyfriends
And yet you let me take your photograph.
He took it back to his atelier
And hung it in the developing room.
I've saved the shot for my wallpaper.

XII

I can't help wanting sex
So near to death – I mean
Geographically. A mere two thousand miles
And the odds on survival drop
Like the mercury drops in me
At some chance word or gesture,
Your face, your look.
I want perfection
But every day the people pass
They have walked for miles
And each of them takes something
Small and dark from our closed garden.
I fear they are taking days.

XIII
You called me 'child'
It was a play-act since
I was wiser than the sea
But after you came home
You stopped, in respect
To the damage done
And called me only
Mother.

Sasha Dugdale

The White Page

Poets don't draw. They unravel their handwriting and then tie it up again, but differently. Jean Cocteau

If you stretch out this writing
into one long, thin single line,
draw it to an invisible thread,

you can make its information
your own material, giving you
the whip-hand over this verse,

this universe – then with a flick
of your wrist, it will ripple into
a silhouette of your own fancy,

a portrait of Widow Wadman
left blank in *Tristram Shandy*
by Sterne for your realisation

in Cixous' ink, or like letters
Molly Bloom sends herself
with love's blind signature.

Ian Duhig

to check the rain

As we stop for a while in the shelter
of a doorway in the thunderstorm
S. holds out his hand
to check the rain.

I'm not sure what more to say about this scene.
Perhaps to say nothing more might be best,
but of course I can't resist.

The hand. The flatness of it. The open-ness. The question of it.
The directness.
The simplicity. The pragmatism. The straightforwardness.
The sunshine that greets his palm.

And maybe just his repetition of this gesture, which must be
  as old as the hills,
as old as the co-presence of hands and rain.

I could probably write about it – that moment, this scene –
and about optimism,
for the rest of my life.

But maybe, like I said, silence,
for now, might be better.

Tim Etchells

In Secret

a response to photographs from Gundula Schulze Eldowy,
Berlin on a Dog's Night: Photographs 1977-1990

... and every word came mended from that tongue
Ralph Waldo Emerson

From the milk pale body of curtained rooms

to the body in its labour
clownface in coal
in oil and steam
in a terrible kiln
on the exhausted bench
making and unmaking the known
looming
on knees
cleaning
emptying
cleaning
emptying
unending as the bricks

between work and the wall lies the wall
walls everywhere the walls

why must we decide ourselves by wounds?

Sunday light
on other days

is a burnished sack of air
we carry to the furthest yard
we can
before it spills

sometimes Sunday light
on Monday still

a still in secret
distilling
the ways out

the earth beneath the ground and then the earth
above it

press

but let us

let us now repair

what do they mean

the things we found and found again

while we waited for the years

to do their worst and then
so tired
to try and do their best

really how

what do they mean

let us repair them while we can

the little bright angel waiting by the gate to the derelict garden

the little dazed angel we carried back on splints of broom

the hand urging us that way not this

the knot of a face

the dog on three legs trying to scent its way in

the rubble and the war buried under it

the wind between the blocks

one or two thin trees

the guilt in the eyes and the joy
in the laced fingers

the abandoned caravan - oh its amputated wheels

the car that turned into a wall and
the wall that turned into a child

the face that searched for directions for
a way out for
the man and the other man who
actually lived

the trolley piled with scraps of the future

the two women who stopped
and are still there

the little girl who inherited her
eyes from a time long before

the razor still sharp after everything
they had seen

the fellow whose cuffs didn't work and whose hair wanted to
leave

the wall that stared at another wall

the working until the lamp gave up and gave
out
and then more
work
this time
the labour of the dark

the sitting right down in a bath of smoke

the holding a dog to the chest like a heart that just happened
to live outside the body

the almost not being able to breathe

the way the hoardings faded but the memories didn't
the way the memories faded but the hoardings didn't

the little man who could just reach the keys

play me something

the shadow of this house on that house

the bed that is never made or unmade

the reflection of the mirror in a shard of water

the thing in the eye no tissue can remove

the place where the road is the destination

the trying to sleep in real night

the drum of one stick waiting for the other

the glass that does not end

the feet that have stopped dancing

the frozen kiss in the wasted alley

the shape of someone sleeping in the bottles

the headless embrace

the mouth that finds the laughing breast

everything one has and nothing
in return

the cosmos of a body on the collapsed sofa

the large tongue that seeks and is found

the stick figures on the door and the stick figures on the street

the cart race without corners

the fading price of silver and of gold

the harvest of crosses in the shadow of the wall

the entire history of a glance
and the sight the century fashions out of tears

the gun barrel luminous as tar

the play gun in the mouth of a cellar

the boys who will always be boys

another gun or the same gun

the leg in the sun-drained window

more smoke building itself
floor
by
floor
out of the ruins

the man and his hat together
on a bench in all the leaves
of the year

the little inky dark angel in its colonnade of lights

a bottle woman gazing at a bottle woman

hands that can touch the past

the coffin of *not yet ready*
of one last
        look
          back

the old Order car with ash on its tyres

a man made faceless with his urge

something like desire emerging out of plaster

'the origin of the world'

semaphore of a dancing arm in air

the wooden horse of landfill slowly rocking
to a stop

***

If we ever leave

on the last train out
past the frayed end of the clock
it is for floodfields
and the solitude of a single bed somewhere between sky
and sky

while trees whisper their beginning
to the fire
and brush their rings
against the mist

and all the things that are
find themselves as close as skin
across the sunken pastures

and while
in the harvested grain of the uncoloured months
a figure from snow approaches a house
stacked out of winter

***

so always
and
again
from the milk pale body of curtained rooms

to the body in its labour
clownface in coal
in oil and steam
in a terrible kiln
on the exhausted bench
making and unmaking the known
looming
on knees
cleaning
emptying
cleaning
emptying
unending as the bricks

and as passing

and as strong

Gareth Evans

Muse

'Write something every day,' she said.
'It will protect you.'

How should this be?
Poetry opens no cell
heals no hurt body

brings back no lover
altogether, poetry is
powerless as grass.

How then should it defend us?
Only by strengthening
our fierce and obstinate centres.

Elaine Feinstein

Looking at Armenian Family Photographs, Turkey, 1915

…this has been bequeathed.

Ghosts in the iris gather around
the eye's disguise of aperture and lens
through whose moist transparency,
film thin, light filters in
to witness seeing,
to see witnessing.

This is the place where
scent too leaves no trace. Touch focuses
fallen blossom, leaf or snow
in silence. History's a miser
of horizons, begrudger
of home, hearth, flame.

This is the day when
the calendar's void instructs no particulars
the refuge of years, deaf and blind
can still touch snaps' smiles and laughter
left behind or hurriedly stashed
to fade beneath others' skies.

This is the man who
thinks the earth's distress
not just intestate dust,
a darkness that feeds on itself
colluding in cleansing memory,
to leave no residue of less or lies or loss.

This is the woman who
remembers shutters' blink, the shots'
echo in the hills over sounds of summer,
sun's saunter down steps pooling blood in a courtyard,
a blade across a face, eyes' vulnerable flesh,
set in the hollows of the bone's witness.

This is the child who this has been bequeathed...

John Fennelly

The bear stands upon its hind legs

for John Berger

Metaphor is needed. Metaphor is temporary.
It does not replace theory.
John Berger

Doubt is the product of a book.

At this point in the film, not believing he'd done it, the interviewer
asks the executive whether the project will harm people?
Everything in the wrong dose will harm people is the reply.

More digging. A fable about nature, that things must be clear to
be understood as though similarly transparent glass is the only
material that'll hold water.

The more the instance, having so many, giving so much, for so
long, the further the misgiving, the wider the cover of cultivation.
But misgiving isn't doubt.

He can't believe he's done it, and keeps digging. Who is she? He
asks. She's the one doing the digging, a tale about nature,
management replies.

A playbook that has worked for ninety years, the most acclaimed
portrayal of the punisher.
Awards, no human presence, masks. The terror in the park. Gutters.

I want to help. A lifetime spent sharing lights, fairly and in square
rubber blocks, giving them to people, neatly, carefully, caring how
they are then stacked up.

SJ Fowler

The Lightkeeper

A night without ships. Foghorns called into walled cloud, and you
still alive, drawn to the light as if it were a fire kept by monks,
darkness once crusted with stars, but now death-dark as you sail
  inward.
Through wild gorse and sea wrack, through heather and torn wool
you ran, pulling me by the hand, so I might see this for once in my life:
the spin and spin of light, the whirring of it, light in search of the lost,
there since the era of fire, era of candles and hollow-wick lamps,
whale oil and solid wick, colza and lard, kerosene and carbide,
the signal fires lighted on this perilous coast in the Tower of Hook.
You say to me stay awake, be like the lens maker who died with his
lungs full of glass, be the yew in blossom when bees swarm, be
their amber cathedral and even the ghosts of Cistercians will be kind
  to you.
In a certain light as after rain, in pearled clouds or the water beyond,
seen or sensed water, sea or lake, you would stop still and gaze out
for a long time. Also when fireflies opened and closed in the pines,
and a star appeared, our only heaven. You taught me to live like this.
That after death it would be as it was before we were born. Nothing
to be afraid. Nothing but happiness as unbearable as the dread
from which it comes. Go toward the light always, be without ships.

Carolyn Forché

Watching *Norte, The End of History* a film by Lav Diaz

I

On the other side of the blind, a bird
is singing. I hear Tagalog for the first time,
how it's a scramble of unexpected consonants,
then U.S. English. The international language
of beer, mobile phones, ATMs and fuck yous;
some things I never knew and other things
I'm reminded of. And all the while the bird
is singing. How much shame there is in being
poor. How secrets are heavy, as hard to drag
along as a squealing pig. There are many myths
about bitter melon. How could you be at peace
with the world's shallowness? Aren't we all only
this much away from weeping on the street?
Is killing a 'bad' person as wrong as killing
someone 'good'? Killing two people the same
as killing one? How eloquent stairs are in shadow,
a woman's face behind a metal grille. I hear
someone eating a bowl of breakfast cereal,
the scrape of a spoon on the ceramic bowl.
The whole row behind me leaves just as a woman
stares at her frothing twin tub. Why can't we
get a grip of our lives? A dog, also watching,
gets restless. A baby purrs on her mother's lap.
The prisoner cleans the floor of a cell he shares
with seven others, one of them playing the guitar,
singing a lullaby. *O my aching heart*
It hurts badly to the core (say the subtitles in bold
white Arial). At night there are cicadas, twinkling
Christmas lights, a bus to Manila. I can't believe
this is a story. I can't believe this is real. The bird
outside might be a swallow. All of us need help,
that's all. When a neon sign says 'It's time to eat',
we stop for Martha's soup and salad, non-specific gossip.

II

Three people lie down, heads raised on pillows. Read
a recipe for cooking snails, 'add corchorus and garlic'.
Four figures, four shadows on a dusty road. Waves
on the shore, a view from above. When you dream
or remember, it goes grainy, out of focus.
Who decided inmates should be called inmates,
wear orange, the colour of joy? A sister calls
her brother in to dinner. The Bible doesn't help.
One makeshift blind comes unstuck – a shaft of light
cast across the screen's top right, dea ex machina,
just what our anti-hero needs. Except it doesn't
stop him fucking his sister like a dog. The wrong man
in prison is an angel, spreading nothing but love,
watering trees, feeding monkeys, kind to thugs.
Although charged, Fate fails to be identified.
Christo brings a ladder to fix the fallen blind.
The dog barks at a big German shepherd on screen.
Two men's lives tied in a cross. The free man
kills the dog called Yumi we thought/he thought
he loved and howls for a long time. Like before,
we don't see the knifed corpse, just the aftermath,
wet blood on his shirt. Four years of absence measured
in four star lanterns, made by hand. You keep thinking
it can't get any worse. Then something else happens.
Slowly. A burning bus, stars scattered, a good man's wife.
The sleeping angel levitates. How do lives like these
end? Goats, hens, children orphaned. Cut to black.
We've forgotten how to talk to each other.

Linda France

Louder but quieter

Parting we step out into the extended hour
when evening continues to draw on the day
and time has a chemical sheen
and space is taken up with slowly concentrating carbonated light.

What else is this but a series of stalled reversals?
Do you trust such colours? Are you listening?

Lavinia Greenlaw

Plums in January, Pen Llŷn

I only bought them as an act of defiance
against winter.
Two little bags left, shivering on the counter,
in the garage shop at Morfa Nefyn –
'50p to clear'.
Dark purple plums.

I don't even like plums much.
But it's the middle of winter, and these had,
somehow, managed to grow and swell
up here on Pen Llŷn,
in our thinness of summer.
So, buying the plaintive fruit, trapped in their plastic bags,
seemed the least I could do.

Getting them home,
driving through squalls of hail drilling the car roof,
I wash them instinctively in a sieve,
then pick the darkest out and take a bite.
Face shriveling before my tongue curls,
furred and sharp as sloe.
Then, smiling at my absurd ambush of surprise,
based on misplaced childhood memories of fruit and nectar,
I start to spit the plum, decapitated now, into the compost,
but something makes me change my mind,
and reaching for the smallest pan instead,
fit the dozen fruit snugly in,
cover with water,
sprinkle some caster sugar on,
and, leaving them to simmer,
go next door to light the fire and read…

An hour later, taking off the lid,
I look into distilled late summer.
The water now alchemised to rubied liquor.
The fruit, skins burst, revealing all below,
in veined and crimson glory –
voluptuous as fuck.

I sip the liquid.
And have to sip again.
Sit down. Closing eyes, to better taste the fruit.
Not bitterness of only an hour before,
now warmth of August on tongue and sun in throat,
transfusing me tonight as
January gales rip against the windows.
I add teaspoons of honey,
and capfuls of vodka,
and eat seven of these jewels in a row.

Five left for later,
batteries against the snow.

Dan Gretton

For John,

with love and gratitude,
and for bringing so many summers into our winters.

Encompassing

No god worth the name would choose a changeless heaven
If he could dip his wings to earth.
Part potter, part poet, divinity flies downwards
And throws clay to sound
An unfurled word –
A thought fired, attracts.

The meaning is in the keening,
The direction of turning,
Tuning the inner ear
To the Earth's magnetic message:
This near-hearted alignment,
Undeniable as gravity or light.

A flit-compass in the swift
Tilts feeling feathers to the field.
The turtle knows its constant way to true.
Even in this torn world, magnetism vouchsafes us:
A geopetal force, an ancient love
Which tugs the lodestone of my soul.

Jay Griffiths

Fingerprints

Look at how we start, like fortune-tellers, at the hands. Here by the
window, where ward meets world, I examine this man's, turn them
over like found leaves. They're remarkable, creaseless, a baby's, glass
palms reflecting my own: now white, now brown. He laughs at my
surprise. A tree surgeon's hands, he says, my skin pressed into other
life, its bark and blood, just like you doc I bet, your fingerprints
handed to others. His hand shakes in mine, shakes mine. I listen to his
heart. Not scared, he says, not of this anyway; but maybe, look, of that
daytime moon, the lit rock of it, what it is, what it means we are. Or
those starlings, did you see this morning? Against the sky like flung
dust. I think our bodies are this, that we merge really, collide and
become the breath of others. Here, he says, go on, have a whiff. My
fingers drum his chest. Did you hear those sounds, he asks, from that
comet, like whale song, mermaids? The ship they landed, its name,
what, Philae? – it means end, or place's edge, some frontier where
things meet. That girl on my street told me when I dropped her a
pound. She's like you, dark-skinned but sodden cold. Will you see her
now on your rounds? Listen to her? It's these distances I regret –
enormous, tiny – their harm. I shine a light in his ears. Hard now to tell
which of us is speaking, where the voice comes from. One of us says
thank you. I go to wash my hands but, seeing them in the water, stop,
turn, return to him.

San Guglani

Words 0

Down the prow
        behind
            them all

She is expectant
        aching
            to be found

Hand to hand
        passed
            from darkness to light

Her white trousers
        cradle
            their unbroken attachment

For a moment he wriggled
        a question
        mark between her thighs

Baby breath
        quietened
            by Mediterranean vernix

The long white thread
        of words
            not his to suck

Like the smallest wave
        the tongue's
            salty prayer dissolved

Mother and child
        become
        288 and 289

The diver's mask fills
            with tears
                        capsized, words drown

Yasmin Gunaratnam

Autumn Here is Magical and Vast

A bloody shaft of light
shone under our door between their compass & the north star
so the road passed through our house out toward the estuary.
Its stones are our tears which silted in our chests until we spat them out.
The road smashed the Janus-faced mirror & flasks of the perfumers
and left us nothing but the clouds to dwell in
with our mouths, as our pockets, stuffed with sand.

***

Rains taught him how he'd evaporate from the earth's body.
The cat taught him how to sleep in the shadows of roses.
The well led him to concealment.
The leaves are going yellow, shouting, whirling about,
so he listens to the pulse of the tree.
The world is tearing through
tatters fluttering like banners in the amphitheatre
where madmen swam in our wounds pleading they'd not heal
nothing will stop all this blood but the sun & the wind.

***

Our dreams remember our dreams.
Like drenched cats we took shelter under the tree when it rained
and big droplets put out our cigarettes.
Flashlights moved across the theatre of clouds.
The hankies were sodden. Chairs were abandoned
where I waited for your hand.
Roots lifted the pavement slabs in front of us
and I concealed your craving on my shoulder
like the tattoo of an unfulfilled desire.

***

The drowned came back with pebbles & the stove was
        black as a burnt pot.
The scissors in your hand are the tail of a dead swallow
& your heart is weaving light shafts & straws as one rug.
The moon of your prayer is full,
it will share its body's loaf with you
& roll like a grindstone of chalk over the cloth of evening.
We will wear what the blind wear,
meanwhile the wrinkles pain raises with its hooves inside your guts
crowd into the corners of your mouth & eyes:
no place but your face.

***

There is a sea tossing & perspiring under the soil,
& a young man is sobbing because he's seen bread. This is your son.
Stretch out your hand & push at this rock with your touch.
From beneath the headstone a thirsting wave comes forth
and places a kiss on the palm of your hand
quiet as this grass, slight as the scarf on your head.

***

If you came back alive to your mother
you would see her tattoos drop blue as perfume,
you would see her mouth's
blood-red cracks,
the names peeling from her salty lips,
you would hear her tongue which made god descend
to smell insomnia's remnants in the rooms' corners.

You would come back
hungered as an idea you're afraid would die
and if you opened any door,
to reassure yourself or to leave,
you would open perplexity.
The mirror would come closer, higher.
Like two old enemies
your eyes gaze into your eyes.

Golan Haji
Translated by *Stephen Watts*

Nuit Blanche

The dark examines us / by touch alone.
John Berger

The talleyman at the door has found your Book of Lies.
Open up to him. He was once your invisible friend,

now he wants to be your ape,
the shade with the diagnosis, your lover's lover.

Creatures in the garden shift position.
Did you see that? No. He mapped it for you

and notated the music that plays to sex and slaughter.
He'll sit it out with you; he'll bring to this long night

long nights of his own, burdens of denial and desertion,
a house subtle with silence, the back-door barricade.

A dreamscape lock-in is bad enough, but now
it's loop-tape encounters with your last lost cause

and memory feeling its way along the wall.
Ask him to put on the light. Ask him to read to you.

David Harsent

an autumn's day

after de Chirico

the avenue of trees
cuts high into the frame

the church's shadow
is black and jealous

we are alive in the sun

time imagines it can stay
I too am deceived

Susan Hibberd

The Laws

ARTICLE 1.
It is solemnly declared: if by the blood of their ancestors they are *strangers* – so shall their children be called *strangers* too –

ARTICLE 2.
And, if so identified as *strangers* – they shall no longer be fit to dwell under the same rough-timbered sky –

ARTICLE 3.
And, if they labour in the cities, they shall no longer reside in the cities; if they live in the country, they shall be deprived of even the wind-scattered sheaves –

ARTICLE 4.
If thus, they find themselves without labour: their idleness shall be punishable;

ARTICLE 5.
And, if the Laws have even once passed judgment upon them: they shall be forbidden speech in the crowded market square –

ARTICLE 6.
If they find themselves without land, wealth or voice: the *stranger* shall live within the pressing confines of the journey –

ARTICLE 7.
Where hours shall be their bread and rustic nightfall their only shelter –

ARTICLE 8.
And if, by chance or destiny, a *stranger* should love a *non-stranger*, they too shall be punished –

ARTICLE 9.

Nor shall they benefit from counsel in the white interrogation rooms.

ARTICLE 10.

Where iron hooks shall be affixed to pillars in Justice's basement.

ARTICLE 11.

And although those in attendance bear false witness, they shall be exempt from forty stripes –

ARTICLE 12.

For no one shall preside over the Laws: *for my beloved, we too are the generation of the Flood.*

Ellen Hinsey

Notes on Love

after Károly Makk's 1971 film, Love

the window glass trembles a peering face
shawled by the arthritic darkness of winter trees

with glass bowl squeal a tram takes the curve
despite a finger-lift of the blind
no-one walks the path

newsprint bleeds through the thin paper
mixing stories of the cold, the cobbles
and the rain that pooled the pitted treads
through afternoons of patient listening

and what of those days grained with waiting?
days that leaked from one to another
in the space of a few flowers placed in a vase
or a door opened and then closed on a sleeping form

they come to this
the greying light of a single bedroom
where a white blouse, trim to a chair
holds a trace of scent too faint for a promise
and a box of odds and ends
letters and half-forgotten books
spectacles, an ivory comb
remains to be found

later, much later
two people will meet here
and there will be
no measure of forgiveness
or accusation or sorrow

he will say:
please, do not tell me
there was no resentment in your waiting
I know how these things fall

and she will wash his body
covering with her hand
the hand of a son
whose forgotten gift
a sprig of forsythia
rests on the table
and drips spring rain
into the scoring of its wood

Graeme Hobbs

A Response to *Here is Where We Meet*

merely duplication of human realisms will never stretch
the human system to its own reaches.
Charles Olson

They come so incessantly, so unavoidable
the new procession, the new rites
a giddying dullness, depthless
in frenzy and foreclosure
The sign diminishes to logo,
cold and clear as the dead
as the calcified white surfaces, empty
but for the steel thicket of lenses.

I know so few in these cities
I cannot read
I do not know how differently I could have done it.

Come from elsewhere, undrawn
the charcoal line cut to paper's edge
A clearing: sudden force of light, conjure
black soil newly turned, silvered
and clump-cut in lunar twilight
The women pivot and gather flints
quiver and hum the body's planes, 'never
before considered another trip'
Easterly, this time
flat to the horizon, on the neck of the earth
Seven hills disclose her curvature

I know nothing of beginnings
but something in the acoustic quality of the air
some track of light, a merging path
a trace cut back urges cadence
odour of sweat in damp fern
spit crackle across air and bone
And now, crossed in the dirt
a mark unfolds, as sign, as mark
The dead recirculate as gift.

I did not know it could be this way, such meetings
that circuits might rupture
Set no course but to wait,
and attend the unbidden
Deterred at first by telegraphic stutter, brusque aside
adjustment sets in, rhythms are caught
and bending to currents of air
we whirl, again, in company
Aloft.

Michael Hrebeniak

More Honour Than

for Ashraf Fayad

More honour than the Wahabi Patrol
More honour than the house of Al Saud
More honour than the oil in the American tanks
More honour than the last $100,000,000 weapon deal with the US
More honour than those who forget the holiness of Palestinian Jerusalem
And the sanctioned swell of the flood of blood
More honour than the chalice in the hand of the king that raised a toast
    with Bush
Bush – the beloved recipient of the shoes of the press
More honour than those who oppress citizens and repress art, love and
    life
More honour than the preachers who practice their immorality in public
without shame
More honour than your 'Divine Will'
More honour than your terrorising powers

If the poet stays in your prison, you will have thousands of Ashrafs
Kept alive forever in our memories and lines
We will track our every move
We will write in the Palestinian
In the language of the lovers we will write
In the language of the Titans we will write
In the language of the activists without getting bored
In the language of the resistance that bides its time

Do not wield the power you hold over your people to attack them or us
Do not offer us a hand or hold up a hand to stop us
Do not put down a Palestinian because we write with our souls

Freedom and life for Ashraf Fayad

Nader Al Hussein

Landfall

When we walk at the coast
and notice, above the sea,
a single ragged swallow
veering towards the earth-
and blossom-scented breeze,
can we allow ourselves to fail

Kathleen Jamie

The Rat King

inspired by Isabelle

The Princess is on the road
But where is the Princess going?
And the beggar – he shouted
My lady, where are you going?
My lady
This is not the right way for you.
She passed by him, hurrying along
Laughing and waving.
She's about to take to the air
On her horses
And she points –
There are rats from the rat kingdom
And the King of the Rats, on two legs
Bearing a crown.
They all salute her white horses.
My apologies, should the wind
Blow them all away
My lady

Abdulkareem Kasid
Translated by the poet and *Ziad Halub;* revised by *John Welch*

Still more marvellous

After your dreams John,
                    when you awake,
         leave traces
         of red

         Speak for those who
         have forgotten

         Tell of the moment
             memories
                 deliverance

In the white church
    a ribbon holds with this single icon

             John
             now I am able
             to be an extra-
             ordinary person
              myself!

Carlos Laforêt
Translated by *Alan Dent*

1
seeing comes before words
see   me   for
       me

2
seeing comes before **words**   seeing comes before **words**
seeing comes before **words**

seeing comes before **words**   seeing comes before **words**
                                 seeing comes before **words**

3
seeing   words
            for
                words

Chris McCabe

Home

I lived at the edge of the town
like a streetlamp whose light bulb
no one ever replaces.
Cobwebs held the walls together,
and sweat our clasped hands.
I hid my teddy bear
in holes in crudely built stone walls
saving him from dreams.

Day and night I made the threshold come alive
returning like a bee that
always returns to the previous flower.
It was a time of peace when I left home:

the bitten apple was not bruised,
on the letter a stamp with an old abandoned house.

From birth I've migrated to quiet places
and voids have clung beneath me
like snow that doesn't know if it belongs
to the earth or to the air.

Nikola Madzirov
Translated by *Peggy* and *Graham W. Reid*

Child Labour

Look at this child
who's learning to read:
she tightens her lips in concentration,
draws forth one word after another,
fishes, and her voice a rod,
eases the line, flexes it and now
lifts these writhing letters
high through the air
so they shine
in the sun of utterance.
so they shine.

Valerio Magrelli
Translated by *Jamie McKendrick*

On the eve of Ferragosto

the accordionist was playing and Guido
whose wife had recently died
was led by his sister

and they two-stepped
slowly around the stage
set up outside the church

under a full white moon
and his son stood watching
watched them dancing

till someone gave him a tube of bubbles
and he drew in his breath
and blew his heart into the wire O

which he held up high
for the wind to blow through
and dancers were turning

in the globules of light
the night wind rose and bubbles
streamed through the wire circle

unstoppable and dancers
stage, church and village all lifted
to meet the white moon.

Caroline Maldonado

Time Consoled in the Stone

I

In the courtyard where sick horses
circle to recover,
a puny youth
his neck thinner than the neck of a sick horse,
stands in the middle of a stone bridge
in long black clothes.
. The censer swinging at his neck
shows how far he must travel,
but his horse is sick,
unable to go
and the moon shall not enter his sleep.

History must move on
and find its place.
The word must find its subject.
His hair must grow long
and be damp and fragrant.

II

Time consoled in the stone
told him,
when it's dark
you'll be driven from here.
But we will remain.
The eagle's beak
snow water
in the well.
Remember your ancestry,
they say history will end
frozen in a photograph.

Man creates his face on his own
and so there is wind.
A place weeping enters our sleep
and never leaves.

*Zeytun/Maraş 1997-8. Zeytun is in the south-east of Turkey, an
area which once had a large Armenian population, subject to
many massacres concluding with the major events of 1915.*

Bejan Matur
Translated by *Ruth Christie*

Goldene Yoykh

Their outer leaves pull off like satin sleeves and the ones
disclosed glisten. Towards their heads, earth, as it always
does, has infiltrated between the skins, so I make a short
vertical cut and flicker through the skins like pages.
John Berger

Night is neither here nor there this new year, a black dog
running against the white. In my hands, Polish wolves return
as newsprint, sniffed, feral, thrilling like satin. The new
government disapproves (of course). Licenses, encloses. Realise
the time. The knife slices through the glistening skins
I riffle and nick. Ribboning, drifts of allium ampeloprasum
dive after allium cepa, milder cousin tagged along & into
hot water. Easy (a short vertical cut) to say *layer* and invoke
family, ethnography, inheritance, mythology, maternity, fairy tales
of peeling back to tribe or DNA. Barley grains. The ones
disclosed glisten; the ones forgotten, names illegible on
daguerreotypes, unspoken by minds passed over, what of
them. Towards their heads, earth. Easier still to say
digging, condensed synthesis of the soup and the poem,
the memory pot ladled, tradition as cellar. Carrots,
ginger: everything rootbodied, brushed from earth. But
not by me. Earth, as it always does, infiltrates
my dreamlife of modernity, crumbs of earth flickering
through the pages of the newspaper read awaiting
a boil. Wolves (they say) pull a blanket of forest after them:
tree weave and deer bone. Bone-in chicken, the cheap
parts for flavour – thigh, wing. A recipe is a story printed on a
tongue, a stock in trade, a tendency. Bones and tendons
of my hands move as hers move, learned without
learning, observed in rebel boredom. I can't draw
but boil and (all elbow) stir, biceps brachii, brachialis,
brachioradialis paddling the wooden spoon against
the tide. Gold 'receives and gives off waves which are not
constant… this irregularity reminds us of living

skin, of a body' (*I Send You This Cadmium Red*). Books
marked by splashed fat. 'Why does everyone want
to *touch*?' Spoon sketches on water, water penetrates spoon,
dyeing the beech darker: tree and its lake reflection. Its
splintered handle pricking thoughts not just of the pencil
but the stake, *palus*, drawing its demarcation. The line that
beckons the threat of overflow. Turn down the heat &
it settles, stillness a myth of simmer, starches breaking down,
proteins realigning. Translucent to opaque, sharp to sweet.
Through the skins, like pages, changes take shape. Can the erasure
of lines be drawn, the melting of flesh and softening? Scats
and prints dark against snow across the Carpathians. Evidence
feathers. Some long-ago ancestor plucked, had pluck, stuck
herself together gelatinous from bone, and so here – glistening
with chicken fat – is where we meet. Night, white bowl, what
splashes between pot and table. Our outer leaves & this inside
remains. Treasure & erasure differ only to a T. Eat, eat. Winter
is a wolf, hot soup; like gold, it will (not) last forever.

Sophie Mayer

My Mother's New Bras

The old pomegranate, storm-hit, propped up
with sticks, sends out a green shoot that goes
straight and up from the root but brings
no hope for the stricken tree. It's the same

for my ninety-year-old mother.
Broken-boned, assisted out of bed, she
goes to the mirrored cupboard, straightens her
back, and takes a long look at herself. Secretly,

she once sent for some cotton bras that
turned out to be a few sizes too big and were
later found among her urinous clothes,
unworn, stiff, in their original folds.

Arvind Krishna Mehrotra

To Write

because the dead can read

because she thought everyone came home to find their family taken

because the one closest to her cannot speak

because he drew love into him from each body he entered

because they are keeping her from him

because the last time they met he misunderstood her absolutely

because a finger can hold a place in a book

because a book rests in a lap

because they recognize each other over huge distances

because he painted the intimate objects of their life together not from observation but from memory; though surrounded by the teacups, the flowers, the garden, he retreated to his small room to paint, each object transformed by love

because we set down what we cannot bear to remember

because words are secrets passed one to another on a train, the same train where Hikmet wrote his poem and where letters were crammed between slats to be found by strangers

because every list poem after Hikmet is an homage

because every true word, everywhere, is samizdat

because belles lettres enrage him

because everything political is personal and not the other way around

because forgiveness is not about the past but the future and needs another word

because the true witness of your soul is sometimes one you've scorned

because it is possible to be married to someone who died many years before we were born

because words are mirrors that set fire to paper

because every day she risked her life for him

because he remembered this too late

because he was mistaken

because he was certain

because certainty and doubt consume each other like dogs in a parable

because of a Sunday morning in London

because of a cemetery in Wales

because of a mountain and a river

because he imagined himself an orphan

because an infant cannot carry herself

because of drawings on fax paper

because she sends her SMS with broken thumbs and an empty battery

because to be heard we do not need a pencil and we do not even need a tongue and we do not even need a body

because the one who holds the pen, even if it's too dark to see the page and even if the ink is his own blood, is free

because an action can never be erased by a word

because we cannot take back what we sang

because the dead can read

Anne Michaels

What are we Talking About ?

for John

What are we talking about?
Of the mountain melancholy and its frozen mists?
Of the legitimate secret of hotel rooms?
Of the train of our days and that of our nights?
Of the hand's line where the book is written?
To be or not to be death's offspring?
Of the hygienic look which washes away all mystery?
Of the shadow chased away by night and iron?
Of the thickness of words against evidence?
Of the great marine ling, of its stormy breath?
Of weathercock minds and squared heads?
Of enemy bows aimed at us?
Of government forever the people's enemy?
Of bourgeois obesity and its sacred fear?
Of Alexander's eagle, Constantine's cross?
Of Noah's dove and Picassos'?
Of bigoted America, slave-owning and murderous?
Of Muslim women condemned from birth?
Of a sign in the sky shining by its absence?
Of clerical hypocrisy, revolutionary virtue?
Of bitter silence and its cold anger?
Of what you must do to die laughing?
Of the stench of the monopolist capitalist State?
Of those whose mouths are bleeding?
Of the vehemence of metallurgical landscapes?
Of a dead letter and another truly alive?
Of tears fleeing into the promised night?
Of the dangerous fraternities of insurgent crowds?
Yes,
Of dangerous fraternity!

Gérard Mordillat
Translated by *Alan Dent*

The White Bear

1

When I first discovered his tracks in the ice-field
        they appeared to have no beginning
and ended in pure black water

without hesitation I knelt down
        and stared into the trembling deep

I saw him swimming through darkness
        with immensely strong and steady strokes
    the violence of his body
redeemed by phosphorescence
        glowing throughout his pelt

        by a slipstream of sand
                and small particles of rock
such as also appears in the night sky
        when meteors are scudding overhead.

2

One day
    in the course of his earthly existence
    he lived in complete solitude eating snow

the next
    he was accompanied by replicas of himself
    grazing the tundra like hogs on a common

one day
    he held his breath underwater for hours
    striking his prey from below like a waterspout

the next
    he had fooled them into thinking his nose
    was the black dot of a meal dosing on the horizon

one day
    he shunted before him ice-blocks the size of cars
    and used them as a shield that made him invisible

the next
    he lifted and hurled these same blocks as easily as dice
    and so crushed his victims or battered their brains out.

3

In the centuries of worship I meant to represent him
    but only managed to carve my own skeleton

I touched him in my mind and prized this connection
    but realised my fear was his greatest gift to me

I regularly ate a part of his body with all due ceremony
    but suffered abysmal headaches and lost patches of my skin.

4

For these reasons among others
    I have chosen not to prevent him
        escaping from me entirely

I have closed my ears and eyes
        when the ice-floes groan
    and glaciers weep their gigantic grief

when the earth stalls and grinds on its axis
    and vaporous purple lights
        stream from its parching gears

I have decided to make a new home for myself
        with hot showers and a table
reliable internet connection
            a wardrobe
    and a lifetime of dry clothes.

Andrew Motion

Naugaja

Last millennium, the generations, with plough and scythe,
      governed by the seasons and the local gods.
A whole way of life bent at the knees in upraised prayer
for the festivals of harvest, Holi and Diwali.
        Each village enshrined in itself.
   So a trek over two mere rivers
 might sea-sicken the barefoot wanderer.

    Thus from their landlocked acres
they were spectres across the passage of conquest
      from Alexander to the Mughals
        unto partition.
Through it all, the elders preached caste
and the folded rites
   where each kept in strict accord with each
 as dictated by the word of a bygone millennium.

    Till the day, men squinted from fields
at a grain in the sky that garnered shadows
    into a giant shape. And watched aswim
     the treasures of Lakshmi
   where her clouds became golden coffers.
Sky unravelling and drifting in a spilled promise
for the eyes of men that were glazed and swept off course
by the gourd of need. *By the surge that sped them*
    for a far off trove that revolved the haven of a foundry
     and swayed their flesh, that phantom,
     hooked on the wield
    of Time and Overtime.

It was not a source of grief. They were spilled in the parallax of
a heavenly guidance seen from earth…that left anywhere
neither here nor there, with all time bereft of beginning or end

    From the furrowed merge of a floor-board sleep
     they were boldened in dreams.
Were flown home on the face of an indigo passport

so they'd pluck the broad-shouldered goddess
of their awed destiny.
They were eye in eye and swank as a rajah
carrying a maharani
to the jasmine scents of their owned
mahaal in the Motherland.

How easy, it must seem, in the absence of a threshold,
for humans to uproot and carry wholesale
their prophets of the air,
their milk and cane of home which abides in the heart
undislodgeable.

Did any of them become household names?
Whose image limelights the mind?
Yet these uneducated tribesmen were pioneers.
With their garlands and bhangra for distant bale dreams,
with their gaudy smiles they refashioned
the cornershops,
made emporium luminous aisles and masala restaurants
open-doors every day across the façade of the Kingdom.
They were a frontier people.

What hurt them?
One day, they felt their flesh and blood
in a language gobbled as the native, with the alien ways
of the sports and the touchy feely dances.
Or saw their lineage torn
by a new-fangled faith that stripped the old word
shawled for the raw new.

They swore to the preacher they'd held a stance
with the children before the whirling incense
of the sacred book
for the far-off rituals. So where was the soul
of the village in their children?
Had the men severed the ancestral bloodline,
their women, under years of the Singer machine, become
bleary,
for this?

The preacher roused spells and potions. Whatever the mantra
for the spells or the potions from whichever new preacher
or the snake priest by the snake shrine,
        still their children
        could not be fathomed.
        Till the father,
        by the gas-work,
        on the way home
        from work, wept.
While the mother lay in the war bunker, in the mind that lay
  in the middle of the garden, and felt again the crossing
             malign her womb.

Were they really here? Were they the husk of a dream?
    Shadows who heard the ghost-force
  of the fathers from the sanded veranda
summoning them home.

We are their offspring and we watched them
        in their haunts. Now one by one in old age
they disappear. I declare their rural values,
        their graft on this soil
and honest toil along with the communal powers
      of Gandhi, who trod these streets,
    are now the enriched values of Great Britain.

Though our children do not speak the foreign tongue
    and though we pour at the hearth mustard oil
      or do not wash our hair on a Thursday
 and though we uphold this or that strange dispensation,
yet may we accept ourselves to claim that a generation past
          with plough and scythe
we were governed by the seasons and the local gods
in a primal village. A village my ancestors called
        Naugaja.

Daljit Nagra

Portraits of my Grandfather .

I

From my birth, Grandfather was always old, toenails
brown and thick hard. To tame them, we first soaked
his feet with valleys deep enough to be a coin bank,
– we joked – in warm salty water and always in the evening
as he sat on his rightful three legged stool, a pouch
of tobacco slinging hip from his waist, his eyes redder
than anything I have ever seen staring down the sun
to set. The old man had a mean tobacco spit on him
that would ricochet across the dirt compound gathering
dust to rest like a landmine, uselessly potent until
naked unsure feet trespassed.

II

One evening, going through an old family album
of photographs with fingerprints and browned unstable
edges, this cannot be him so young. I refuse to give him
youth but his eyes- even in this black and white photograph
they are redder than anything I have ever seen.
That is my grandmother beside him, short, very close
to the earth, beautiful. The year at the back still boldly
in print, 1939. This they stand on used to be their land
I will learn later, but history back then did not have prophecy.
For now, they stand on their land, hand in hand, pregnant
and with hope as they used to say in the English Mission
Schools.

III

Somewhere in Burma, group photograph black and white
of black soldiers, he leans into his rifle eyes peering out
of India to ask how many types of men there are that some
die for others. Here as well at home, freedom never wore
the colour of his skin and white doves do not own peace.
It is in Burma that he learns the secret to the white man,
That he too bleeds and dies. When he comes back to find
his land gone, his home, a village surrounded by spiked
trenches, he will reveal his secret to many and they go deep
into the forest to make guns and war. From here onwards
he begins to look old. This is the grandfather I have known.

IV

Next one, is of my grandmother, close to the earth, harvesting
maize, her son strapped on her back like a hump. More and more
she is appearing alone, her husband, a warrior at war. Cucu, tell
us a story, 'Once there was blacksmith who went far away
to smith, he left his beautiful pregnant wife behind, an ogre
occupied their home, she fed a friendly dove castor nuts and oiled
it wings, the dove traveled far, far, far into the country to sing
the news to her husband. He came home and killed the ogre
with a sword he carved himself'. The child on Cucu's back
will go to the forest as well, and she will carry guns and bullets
to him like mother's milk.

V

Grandfather in the forest, with him men and women dread-
locked to the shoulders, there is laughter and smiles, home-
made guns and captured grenades in their arms, sitting
on Grandfathers lap one day, he would tell me twice
he tasted freedom, as a child and in the forest. The year
of the photograph in fading lead, 1962, one year before
independence, victory was at hand, there was much
to celebrate. But in 1963, he was to leave the forest
to find history was a revolving wheel, black was white.
He was to spend the rest of his life in chains that wore
the colour of his skin, the secret of the dove failed him after all.

V1

He died years before Cucu and where he went, no doves
can reach him. We buried him with his tobacco pouch
hanging hip from his waist. In this photograph, Cucu
is throwing soil over his grave. Her son is not here,
he is in jail and when they tell him he must wear chains
to bury his father, he refuses, not even for death will he wear
chains. Cucu doesn't mourn for him but for us, she says
'I have known love and freedom, I wish them for you as well'
The year of the photograph is 1978, a few months before
the first President's death.

VII

'Nothing changes, we take turns dying, even hope'
is all she says after egalitarian Alzheimer's has leveled
all of us nameless. Then she remembers my father and says
'except for my son, he will find freedom for you, just wait
and see.' My grandfather, used to say, 'do not straddle
the earth and the grave, chose one and live with it damn it!,
If I could, I would go back to the forest for you nitwits,
did I give birth to men or girls?' To which my Grandmother
would say 'As if we women were not in the trenches. Do you
even know how many times I was arrested? Leave them alone,
their time will come.' This last photograph, a family portrait.

Mukoma Wa Ngugi

three ways of seeing

in homage to John Berger

1 Ilkle

the Romans took this hill
you peacefully climb
just a scuffle with the mist
a downed carnation

autumn is fortified
in its fierce revolt against the green
snow is a metal
skilled at flowering in nightfall

rumpled immensity
                    unreachable stillness
though nothing remains

only a bas-relief rusty
what others refused to see
and space stirs up

2 Tahiti

I saw a blue tree and painted it
an indigenous woman with red hips
and a yellow cloudscape falling to pieces as well
reality like coconut milk

drunk in a starless night
they're primary colours
                              nothing to be afraid of
less false than gold

or everything hung in Orsay Station
my tomb is real
                         mouldy slab

among sparkling vanities
on my stiletto Van Gogh's ear
in my soul syphilis

3 Montparnasse

traveler notebook
with its endless graph paper
parts from all parts
the gypsy woman who begs unlooking

yet always sees you
the rat on the rail
gnawing on high voltage lines
the aphonic accordion

          sitting down to laugh
real unreal scenes
heartby the fireside

          disheveled reason
off the metro nothing
          leftward whole

Víctor Rodríguez Núñez
Translated by *Katherine M. Hedeen*

The Rain it Raineth

Its murder out. It's raining fog and darkness.
It's like a cancelled fixture
In the Third Division North
In 1954, where Nelson will not now
Be entertaining Barrow.
High in the bare trees, the crows
Are laughing it off. *Haw haw.*
Back when the crows were henchmen –
As their greasy midnight coats attest –
Out doing knifework for the Duke
It rained for pitch-black centuries.
Huizinga said men thought it was the end
And climbed into their coffins to prepare.
The crows well knew that it was just another
Slow catastrophe like this – *haw, haw* –
The weather, economics,
General bastardy. So *plus ça change,*
The crows declare and cackle in the rain.
So *plus ça* fucking *change. Haw haw.*
And next time out we might be bankers.

Sean O'Brien

In official histories

the leaving one
never wrote about the lover

There's just an old bruise
that will not leave them
beside the heart

a doctor pauses
at the colouration

he sees these all the time.

A flare of sunlight on someone's
arm on a bus, and that man looks up
to a face with sudden hope,

as if her before she met him
so joyous, her full laugh,
her skin almost without thought

He keeps hearing of women
who walk into marriages with
a sense of fate, with absolute hesitation,

Those who leave
And the ones left
recognise such histories,

they can perceive the flirt in a dance
beneath its camouflage,
certain as a wink or billet-doux.

Some poems go nowhere,
you just keep unrolling the maps of love

Michael Ondaatje

The Wild One

Johannes Vermeer, *The Art of Painting*

She stands beside a death mask under a chandelier,
head turning from an unseen source of light.
She's holding a leather Thucydides
and a seventeenth-century trumpet
without piston, slide or valve
as if she doesn't know what to do with it
and might prefer a lute. On the map behind

South is torn from North, the West on top,
East nowhere. On the canvas, all that shows
are glaucous leaves of laurel for her hair.
The real picture, the one Vermeer never sold
even at his poorest, is himself – painting History
in disguise as a maenad. We might take her hand,
step her down from the frame,

dress her in jeans and a T-shirt, open those eyes.
She's not a scholar collating an archive
though she'll help if they're fair, nor a journalist
after a story, twisting what's said to make scandal,
sell. Though she's on their side too, if they mean well.
She's blood from the heart's right ventricle,
witness and balance, sift, record and judge.

Her name Clio comes from glory, telling
glorious things we did. But she's a wild one!
Look at her – making us feel out of depth
or guilty for not listening. Oh, she's foul play.
She's dust on a galactic nebula, nothing to do
with today. She'll spend centuries name-checked
and dismissed. *History's bunk*. But she's all there is.

Ruth Padel

Brood

At sixteen, I did a day's work
on an egg farm. A tin shed
the size of a hanger.

Inside its oven dark
two thousand stacked cages,
engines of clatter and squawk.

My job, to sift a torch
through the library of bars
for the dead hens

and pack a bin bag
until it was tight as a pillow.
All the time my mind chanting

*there's only one hen.
Just one ruined hen repeated
over and over.*

In this way I soothed
the sight of all that caged
battery, their feathers

stripped to stems,
their wings like grills,
their patches of scrotum skin.

But what kept me awake
That hot night in my box room,
as I listened to the brook outside

chew on its stones and the fox's
human scream, was how
those thousand-thousand birds

had watched me. And really
it was me repeated over and over,
set in the amber of their eyes.

Me, the frightened boy in jeans
stiff with chicken shit, carrying
a bin bag full of small movement.

A foot that opened. An eyelid
that unshelled its blind nut.
A beak mouthing a word.

Mark Pajak

the dead are with us
John Berger

the dead   do not

stumble into dream
casual & causal as lit
cigarettes burning regret

down to the stub they
become as they turn
& look trying to

say what in life they
never did : nor do they
pose in celluloid frames

– those reeling iterations
of near-identical ghost
nor can they speak

past words written
while still breathful or
from under sheets folded

neatly into envelopes
to be scissored open
at their un-creation

nor do nervous im-
pressions in chunks of
brain bring them singing

back as though from fronts
whose far bombshells
nightly rumble us

a shallow ocean away
nor is there day or hour
when membrane thins &

that thin pulse bleeds through
to summer gardens slanted
with yellow light where

we find us all at once
not quite alone : no
they simply are

the dead
with nothing
of us no purpose

& that means to
progress with
-out us all

their own

Mario Petrucci

February 26, 2012/In Memory of Trayvon Martin

Script for Situation video created in collaboration with
John Lucas

My brothers are notorious. They have not been to prison. They have been imprisoned. The prison is not a place you enter. It is no place. My brothers are notorious. They do regular things, like wait. On my birthday they say my name. They will never forget that we are named. What is that memory?

The days of our childhood together were steep steps into a collapsing mind. It looked like we rescued ourselves, were rescued. Then there are these days, each day of our adult lives. They will never forget our way through, these brothers, each brother, my brother, dear brother, my dearest brothers, dear heart –

Your hearts are broken. This is not a secret though there are secrets. And as yet I do not understand how my own sorrow has turned into my brothers' hearts. The hearts of my brothers are broken. If I knew another way to be, I would call up a brother, I would hear myself saying, my brother, dear brother, my dearest brothers, dear heart –

On the tip of a tongue one note following another is another path, another dawn where the pink sky is the bloodshot of struck, of sleepless, of sorry, of senseless, shush. Those years of and before me and my brothers, the years of passage, plantation, migration, of Jim Crow segregation, of poverty, inner cities, profiling, of one in three, two jobs, boy, hey boy, each a felony, accumulate into the hours inside our lives where we are all caught hanging, the rope inside us, the tree inside us, its roots our limbs, a throat sliced through and when we open our mouth to speak, blossoms, o blossoms, no place coming out, brother, dear brother, that kind of blue. The sky is the silence of brothers all the days leading up to my call.

If I called I'd say good-bye before I broke the good-bye. I say good-bye before anyone can hang up. Don't hang up. My brother hangs up though he is there. I keep talking. The talk keeps him there. The sky is blue, kind of blue. The day is hot. Is it cold? Are you cold? It does get cool. Is it cool? Are you cool?

My brother is completed by sky. The sky is his silence. Eventually, he says, it is raining. It is raining down. It was raining. It stopped raining. It is raining down. He won't hang up. He's there, he's there but he's hung up though he is there. Good-bye, I say. I break the good-bye. I say good-bye before anyone can hang up, don't hang up. Wait with me. Wait with me though the waiting might be the call of good-byes.

Claudia Rankine

On Stage

The Royal Court, Katrin full on in us,
like thunder cooking in our arteries,
her death a time-slip error, quantum flip
into 4-D; I'd gone looking for her
as same street culture-assassins, the rip
in time, like carjacking gloss polymer,

and played Bowie's 'Five Years' to stabilise,
his faggy, dystopian falsetto
calling on urban aliens to come out.
We coded matching purple shoe laces
one dusty summer, each black pointy snout
like nerve endings, and hung out in places

on Hampstead Heath, she read my books for parts
in which she'd reverse sex, subvert the lot
into uninhibited androgyny.
She'd go so deep mining a character
I'd meet her stoned on new identity
looping our street, like tasting a flavour.

And John, our hot hormonal energies
brought to the stage the last human despair
of absent contact, words as substitute
for Katrin sucked clean out of a window
into tomorrow as another shape
of consciousness, enormous as the glow

of a big lemon sun, and we embraced
supportively, both energised by loss
to fill the moment, I recall your hand
so aesthetic, so earthy, folding mine
implicitly, like we made a last stand
to give her moving on a little shine.

Jeremy Reed

94/365

let me write this poem from a distance
the distance of knowing nothing of you
nothing of your mind nothing of your heart
from knowing only that you are present
from the feeling that these lines are your lines
lines to allow you to observe yourself
from a distance knowing nothing of me

all I am is what I'm doing right now
trying to meet a stranger late at night
when the only thing we have in common
is an unpredictable attraction
that for some reason neither of us wants
to break quite yet

each of us curious
and only modestly exploitative
of the other and both smiling trembling

Angus Reid

Storm, Nissaki

The sky claps once, then throws itself open; the room
flares wide and white

and jolts sideways, jumping the rails.
Sheet lightning – lighting the night to *before*

and *after*: after-images of black and white.
At each flash the room leaps, across itself

to the other side, from a black box to a box of light. The sky
opens its hands and claps them shut; thunder stoops

to shiver the house's great stone bell. Another strike
takes a snapshot of me, there on the jetty; an epileptic

kick of lightning and I'm scribbled out clear –
this pale, forked nib of a life.

The room sits up suddenly, bright as a photo-booth,
then turns on its side like the sea.

Robin Robertson

Homewards

That England is populated will always come as a surprise;
humans can live on an island only by forgetting what an
island represents.
Giles Deleuze, *Desert Islands*

I had never handled a tool in my life; and yet, in time, by
labour, application, and contrivance, I found at last that I
wanted nothing but I could have made it, especially if I
had had tools.
Daniel Defoe, *Robinson Crusoe*

The sea so far away seeming, always,
beyond sands clagged to wind-carved dunes,
slack salted with marram, wort and worry.

Waves arrive from who knows where,
the flat edge of the unknown slipped
beneath our door, a last note unfound

whose words spread to let roots cling.
Thrift gathers marbled bells of red and pink,
strung out for the wind to chime.

The oceans did not need to rise,
left us what once we worked so hard.
All gone to mud and dry now,

to someday crack, water rivering
into new lakes, slopes and knolls,
villages creeping solidly downhill.

So far from sea and nowhere, still.
A simple place to live, a stack
of logs set to dry for burning

a fire for ache and tired talk,
miraculously strange tongues
made powerful by company,

the craft of our walking and talking
a place into being, our only home
the hearth of the yards ahead of us.

Mark Robinson

Who was a Communist?

My parents didn't tell us which of their friends and relations
were Communists and which weren't,
so we had to do it ourselves.
A group of teachers and their partners came over
from my father's school,
Len got out his guitar and they sang,
'I'm the man, the very fat man who waters the workers' beer'.
They must be Communists, I thought.
A group of teachers came over from my mother's school,
and a man called Wally told stories about an engraving firm
controlled by 'the masons', he said.
My dad was fascinated by Wally's stories and kept saying,
'Christ, would you believe it?!'
So I asked my mum if Wally was a Communist
and she said, 'Of course not, you mustn't ever say that.'
Then we went on a camp with the Hornsey Communists
and a woman spilt meths on her groundsheet
and it burst in to flame.
My dad said she was a bloody fool
so I reckoned that though she might have been a
Communist once
she wasn't one now.
We went camping with Fred and Lorna,
and when we sang 'I'm the man the very fat man
who waters the workers' beer' Lorna didn't join in
and said, 'Oh Fred, come on, there's no need to
sing that one,' so Lorna, I thought, was not very Communist.
Sometimes we went to see two families who
lived upstairs and downstairs in a house.
Upstairs was Francis the Armenian who was so Communist
quite often he wasn't there – he was working for peace
in Czechoslovakia. Peggy, his wife, though
was very Communist, I thought, because
she not only talked about peace, she talked about
peace-loving peoples.

My father said that she sounded like a bloody gramophone
record, but as we often used to listen to bloody gramophone
records of the Red Army, I didn't know why there
could be anything wrong with that.
Downstairs there was Roy who was the most miserable
man I have ever known. Even his hands was miserable.
He said that everything was bad. As my parents
said some things (but not everything) were bad as well,
it was possible, I thought,
Roy was more Communist than them.
Roy's wife, was sometimes ill and had to go to bed for
months. But when she came out of the bedroom
she was very smiley and seemed to say that
everything wasn't as bad as Roy said it was.
I wasn't sure if that meant she was more or less
Communist than Roy.
There was Moishe and Rene who weren't just
Communists they were almost my parents.
Moishe went to school with my father and
Rene went to school with my mother.
They had even camped together.
When they talked it was like they were
a moishe-rene-my mother-my father Communist camping club.
Then there were the relatives or 'meshpukkhe' as
my father called them.
My father's mother was so old and so Communist, she was the first
Communist. And her father they said, was a
Communist-before-there-even-were-Communists.
My mother's mother, 'Bubbe', kept
chickens and said the woman who did the 'bag wash'
was trying to diddle her. My father said that she
wasn't a Communist, she just 'kvetshed' (complained)
but she made the best shmatena (a kind of yoghurt)
in London so maybe that made her some kind of
a Communist without knowing she was.
I asked my mother if 'Zeyde' (her father) was a
Communist and she said very angrily that he was
'some kind of Trotskyist'.

That sounded terrible. And yet he was so nice.
He took me to Hackney Downs where he
showed me to his friends who said, every time,
'Is that your Grandson, Frank?'
'Yes,' he said every time,
'He's a nice looking boy,' they said every time,
and went on talking in Yiddish.
As I didn't speak Yiddish I had no way of knowing
whether they were Trotskyists too.
In 1957, we went to Communist East Germany
and there was a row between everybody on the
delegation about whether Stalinallee (Stalin Alley)
looked like a public lavatory or not.
We saw the Carl Zeiss camera works,
Frederick the Great's house,
Goethe's house, Schiller's house, Bach's house,
Luther's castle, Buchenwald concentration camp
and Hitler's bunker.
When we got back, my parents stopped being
Communists.
They called me and my brother in and said
that they didn't agree with the Communist Party
and democracy.
I had no idea what that meant. Not a clue.
The ones who were Communists went on being
Communists and now we weren't Communists.
Every so often Roy came over and said
everything was getting worse.

Michael Rosen

Cuckoo

Over and over
the cuckoo calls
down the long slopes her strange
two-note call

falling with the long light
down the slopes
two falling notes that sound
like the measure

of us or like something
that the fields
remember something that happened
on these slopes

where the farms gather
and disperse
this long spring light where trees
fill with it

the cross in the church
remembers them
Labout in his hat
and crooked collar

Farges who smiled
for the camera
Peret who came down
from the hill

when the first walnuts
were falling like leaves
in the family
orchard each man

with his particular
way of moving
whose body knew this place
learning itself

as it learnt the place
that it was made
to measure itself by
but being called

away left the long slope
left the orchard
and left the sheep
under the walnut trees.

Fiona Sampson

I long to walk

I long to walk
by a big river
its strong slow sweep
carrying my story away
but the craving of my kind
has remade the world
in its own crooked image
and the signs all around
say only:
this *is* your story
Though the world is innocent
it can no longer
cleanse our guilt
there is a time for regret
and a time to transcend our own kind
and it is now
though it is late

Clare Sandal

All That is Solid

Gon: Here is everything advantageous to life.
Ant. True; save means to live.
Shakespeare, *The Tempest*

1

all that is solid melts into air
the great globe itself
dissolves,
all that is holy is profaned

heavenly highs,
cloud-capped corporations,
idyllic Ponzi schemes,
the postcolonial seminars
of neocolonial regimes

all gone, *kaput*

so melancholy Prospero
retiring from the tiny island
that saved him *it was*
after all, only a stage
is reduced to living
in his own skin

there is no island,
no stage

no spirit slave

& gone is Caliban,
bad breath gone,
excruciated teeth,
his disabused truth
no less self-absorbed

than the true gobbledegoo
of Prospero's motley crew

the whole bunch
went out & got
drowndéd in the icy waters
of egotistical calculation.

2
. . . gone & left
drifting impassioned over them
the wrack of a still youthful Marx,
the species drama of the *Manifesto*
poignant in its nakedness, catching
a rhetorical lift on the long withdrawing
wash of *The Tempest* —

a grand gesture to usher in
the anguish of the age
we ourselves live & will surely
die in: compelled to face
the real conditions of our life
& our relations with our kind . . .

we who imagined no world
other, than what we fell into,
stupefied   *hardly believing*
what was *happening* is *happening*
even as we are even now

plunged

into the sea of wreckage & plunder
that long ago imagined us

James Scully

Stateless Passport

SEVEN SISTERS express their milk & sap into the New River
Joseph Conrad posted through a dark slit
paddling from Tollington Park: *the horror, the horror*

Bethune Road where an orthodox man becomes a cakestand
supporting a fur wheel on his head, heading south, Manor Road,
St Anne's House, fat mattress, vagrant bride, shiny black bags
of the o so recently dead, Third Eyes under gables of
suburban villas, Bouverie Road, marooned sea cadets
carousing with Daniel, Defoe Road, where the book says
'every work of fiction must owe a lot to the author's experience'

WOOD PULP invades our veins & a hollow log, burnt and scraped,
becomes a funerary barge. Viking raiders foiled
when Alfred dammed Blackwall and stole the broad Lea.
Walthamstow Marshes, adder's tongue fern, common comfrey
fattening weary kine, Lea Bridge Road, Millfields, Cornthwaite,
Thistlewaite, Lower Clapton, Cricketfield Road, at the weary trudge
Norfolk geese and drovers on their sanctioned routes.
Downs again, Pembury Road, drawn to crackle of riotous radio,
a chartered welcome where tavern burns at theoretical centre

WHEN civic necklace breaks, pearls lodge in your throat

Iain Sinclair

'Fabiola'

for John Berger

A crimson veil and a paling face,
a figure straight out of a Book of Hours.
Moments of goodness are time machines
and beautiful eyes are telescopes to the unseen.

To see and the want to know are the same
– memory is just another way of knowing –
but I cannot recognise these three faces,
lowered, louvered and heavily modified.

Depth cannot be found in a single image,
but placed together, they move from space to time.
I have to look at many to see just one
and forever is space-bound, not found in time.

We only grasp things juxtaposed in clusters,
a mess of spilled materials, a cosmos.
A fuller grasp comes when all is brought to rest,
no longer fixed to the flux or the *durée*.

By setting the replica over the original,
what is lost is not time but the aura.
In the eyes of the creator, viewed *en masse*,
the true face is the stereoscopic view.

Richard Skinner

Matuska Speaks

'When God and Kaiser the order gave,
Hundreds I annihilated.
Then they called it an "offensive."
No one asked about a motive,
And twice I was even decorated.
Then I did the same thing privately,
Suddenly they called it beastly!

All round they shout "Heil Hitler!" daily.
The guy keeps getting, right to order,
From Thyssen, Skoda chunks of money.
Why? He'd set the people free.
And how? Simple: through mass murder!
I did the same. None cries out fiercely,
"Heil Matuska!" No, it's jail for me.

There's two kinds of mass murderer:
One they call a criminal,
The other without demur,
They promote to general.

Of the two, who's more gaga,
The world itself or old Matuska?'

Jura Soyfer (1912-1939)
Translated by *Wolfgang Görtschacher* & *David Malcolm*

*Szilveszter Matuska (1892-1945) was a Hungarian mass
murderer and mechanical engineer who made two successful
and at least two unsuccessful attempts to derail passenger trains
in Hungary, Germany and Austria in 1930 and 1931.*

from 'Origins:
Stories told to me by Helen and France'

Their mother, Manon
Dordogne Valley
Occupied France, 1943

      In a cave
so dark they touch to see,
Manon is born.

Beside the Dordogne River, smell
of fresh water seeps
through dust into the narrow
slit in the cliff
behind the neighbour's house.
We climb here when we can.
Movement is dangerous.
Through the last months of the occupation
the neighbours carry bread, a bowl with whatever
water is not lost to the hillside,
they bring fruit, mashed for the baby
who cannot see the bright colour,
can only taste vividness.

Manon does not learn to use
her eyes – so little light.
(*Every light is a risk*
for you. For us.)

Paintings fifteen thousand years old, animals
in every pose
mobile, floating over her crib.

Though it isn't possible, her eyes
shut all those months, Manon
remembered the paintings,
Told Helen and France about the bison,
reindeer, horse, ibex
limned onto the cave's side
in ochre stirred with saliva
sometimes painted, sometimes sprayed
by the human mouth,
or a thin tube like a whistle.

(The whole artist's trible jointly laboured,
jointly imagined, visions mingling
in chalk-dust, red as dried blood,
brown as the earth of hills.
They gathered around a single wick burning
in hollowed stone, walnut oil.)

Manon's blank eyes, the colour won't blossom
in them without light. A rag
stuffed in her mouth to stop her cries.
Her only language: milk, the bright
sweetness of fruit.

Esta Spalding

Syrian Artist

You talk of small graves
you've seen, stones –
rubble really – piled
pitifully, no time for ritual
in Syria; and you recreate them here
in Europe, on a city street,
with your supple artist's hands,
forlorn paintings nestled
in the chill core of each,
homage to child after child,
after child.

An old Polish woman walks by, her eyes
full of graves from another war.
She opens her purse, gives you half
its meagre contents: 'For the children,'
she says, pressing a few coins
into your palm, insistent. Coins
and stones, stones and coins,
gathered, heaped and shattered,
again and again, and again;
and always children
in their midst.

Gerda Stevenson

After the Mowing

I

The season of the cut and clear. The bales squared
in the distance, a hollow house, no windows or doors.

The Ns of the fence posts, perforated shadows.
The cupped sky, inverted. A sense of limit

in parallel lines, with no convergence in
the distance. The local held fast beneath

a vastness. I thought of the struggle against the angel
and the struggle against a stump, for the deepest roots

go into sky and earth alike. What arms
and rods can pry them? Inaudible,

oh why
do you ask my name?

The smallest meet
the fiercest teeth and claws
with soft mouth and
velvet paw.

Invisible, farther,
the ax against the grain, bounced back,
ringing, from the heartwood's iron.

II

The wind was coming from the East,

toward me, holding

each vertical lightly on

its leash. Then slowly,

stillness

    and a rustling,

the fence posts now

near enough

to touch.

    There at the top of each, a massed

        form of

(slick gradations, brown, black, and gray

like wadded swathes of

taffeta,

        creased and folded,

           tectonic,

              fanned, unfolding,

then stiffening, anamorphic)

quills and feathers

now snapped

out, awakened, doubled shapes awakened

        and change, changing,

                into the full sweep of wings

into lift and speed, the air already churning

            at their tips –

It seemed the earth, too, was tossing like the sea

            as the great hawks rose,

            a pair,

                and dipped, circled,

                climbed into

the high flow,

the wind's

road, gone,

as two,

each alone.

III

to the *Nth*, like the truth of an ending
unskeined across the crust of the white field.
Though it happened only once, I
am sending the thought
of the thought
continuing.
To return to
the field before the mowing.
When a goldfinch swayed
on a bluestem stalk,
and the wind and the sun
stirred the hay.

Susan Stewart

Tongue

The tongue is alone and tethered in its mouth
John Berger

The man in front of me
is reading
a balance sheet

He is smiling, his gaze
shimmying between columns
effortlessly
bilingual

And though a little drunk
on the liquor of profit

I like to think he is not immune
to the sharp beauty

of integers, simmering
with their own inner life

and I wonder if he feels
the way I do sometimes
   around words

wishing they could lead me
past the shudder
   of tap root
      past the inkiness
         of water
                          to those places

where all tongues meet

         calculus Persian Kokborok flamenco

the tongue sparrows know, and accountants,
and those palm trees at the far end
of holiday photographs

  your tongue
  mine

the kiss that knows
from where the first songs sprang

  forested and densely plural

the kiss
that knows
no separation

Arundhathi Subramaniam

ligne rouge

draw me a line
blunt in this sand

all form dictated
by the weight of days

fluid & free-wristed
the bulge of our losses

a love underscored
an error struck-through

the limb of each draught
made sure & unflinching

the awkward curve
of truth's gaunt lips

the flush of the liminal
in cadmium red

Paul Summers

Orison

Each rescue has its list, as painters knew:
Annunciation never simply girl in garden,
Winged man on his knees, it needed

Comb and needle, lily, apple, mirror moon.
Beyond the garden, darkest forest,
Leaves and branches curling in the heat.

For some, accoutrements are telephones or sun,
A touch, kiss, drink. It may be hard
To pick a moment when you cross the line.

Yet always away offstage is that roar
Of flame, the fuselage of all that's past,
Torn open like a blackened wound.

O pilot cast as smithereens, navigator lost
I pine straw. God of rescue, withhold not.
O come. We are waiting for our future.

Michael Symmons Roberts

Photograph at a Table

Truths... are born – sometimes late
John Berger

Truth is the voice, said voice. *No, truth is skin,*
said skin. *All truth is two-faced,* Janus said.
The photograph stayed silent, dense yet thin.
The living were all living yet were dead.
The face looks out and reads itself as me,
the viewer said, recalling what she saw.
I was that child and never can be free
of what I was, the adult said. *It's awe*
of things, the body whispered in the bone.
It is existence elsewhere, said the text
on the blank page. *It is being alone,*
said the stars, *neither before nor next.*
I am, said the editor. *I'm both 'and' and 'but'.*
I frame, said the eye. *I open and I shut.*

*

So she was sitting there and still she sits
at the same table where the moment landed.
I knew her, he said. *Look how the moment fits.*
The hopeless yearning gaze that once attended
all her moments is preserved in light
and form. It's simply how the cards are dealt
as well she knew when she swam through the night
before arriving here with what she felt
was hers. Her life is re-disposed around
the moment and is thereby recognised
as what she knew and knows. And so she found
herself as fixed and frozen and downsized.
Mama, cried time. *How strange to find you here!*
The furthest away, oddly the most near.

*

The being here, the having been, the trace
of self, the formal presence - even this
apparently strict sonnet pulls a face.
Remember me and touch me with a kiss,
the moment pleads, its breath misting the glass.
Truth is the glass and breath at once. Breathe out,
become imagination, be as grass
and air, as weather. Become the half-heard shout
in the street and keep becoming. Fix time now.
I hold your photograph. It's where you live
and vanish yet remain, I don't know how.
It is the place from which you might forgive
this hopeless distance. It's the form of things.
It can't talk anymore and yet it sings.

George Szirtes

Decembrance

A clear, cold, windless break of day
enlightens sherbet tiles, frosted trees,
candied webs on webs of twigs and
candid fields of grass and fallen leaves.

Smoke's the only motion in the still:
fat squirrel tails unfurl themselves
from chimneys; cross-modal echoes of
the stock-dove's fluffed up grey asides.

Someone has lit a fire to unpack time
from Nature's stasis, where growth and rot
are both on pause, flames unravelling
the Summer's logged alluvium

compiled from stifling afternoons when
leaf-sipped light married
leaf-inspired air to root-sucked damp.
How brief it was, how brief!

Raymond Tallis

The Fish

for Marie-H Desestré

The whale glides on the water's surface
like a loose platform
like a cathedral adrift.
It does not have the face of a cetacean
it is more like a swollen moray eel
with a projecting lower jaw,
a gargoyle derived from the future demolition regime.
Through the river's mouth
it draws its enormous lack of understanding
with the serenity of an enigma
or the obstinacy of a bat.
Hence the cracks in its flesh
and the strips of skin hanging from its sides,
hence its temporary solitude, its apathetic solitude.
It is the dream of a night
imposed by the fishbone of a poem
like the mark of a scratch the origin of which we forget,
and of a walk we never took
except around the whale,
an attraction diving and emerging
from the waters of a bay, cut out
and pasted on a piece of paper, surrounded
by the rubble of a conversation
which remained incomplete.

Eli Tolaretxipi
Translated by *Philip Jenkins*

Seville, 21st century

He was on top form indeed
that day in Seville Cathedral.
The guide took them first to the Giralda,
gave them an hour to go up and down
and buy the necessary souvenirs.
After that he hustled them into the temple;
next to the so-called 'Tomb of Columbus'
he showed them the templa and the statues
and gave them his usual spiel:
The angels' tears, for instance, are Guatemalan sapphires,
The Madonna's tears are Bolivian rubies
and the whole organ is made from Tahitian wood,
and so on and so forth.
It was then, just after the Tahitian wood,
that our guy interrupted the guide:

'Imagine villages getting burned,
women and babies burning in the flames,
babies being sold in the slave trade,
being buried alive in mines.
Imagine a consumptive child being thrown off a cliff
because it can't work anymore.
Your Cathedrals are built of this child's blood
Your Madonna's tears are made of the blood of the
slaughtered...'

His words created a buzz;
Everybody in the group agreed – they couldn't do otherwise
and the bored guide shut his mouth
(it's not as if he didn't want to).
'Of course, you are right, you are right, my fellow...'
they'd tell him one after another in the restaurant where they
          were taken for lunch
(yes, even the retired teacher with his wife
and the young entrepreneur who was on his honeymoon),

'Colonialists were this and that…'
And his friends – they couldn't have congratulated him more
if he had succeeded in the University entrance examinations.
'You told them off nice and good, dude,' (it was certain that he
    had told someone off).
And so bottles of beer and sangria kept coming.

And it goes without saying that he was feeling self-satisfied;
He had stolen the show with just a few words
and now he was enjoying the lovely noon
in the Sevillean restaurant –
they say that if you haven't seen Seville at noon, you haven't
    seen Heaven…

Later on he wanted to take a piss (too many beers, you see).
In the toilet a cleaner was mopping,
she was probably from Morocco or somewhere,
dried up, her skinny cheekbones protruding,
she stood aside to let the customer pass.
He walked on the wet floor
and afterwards, when he pissed – his flow was irregular –
    half of his urine wet the floor.
Never mind – the cleaner would take care of it.
When he had finished relieving himself he opened the door
walked by her as if she were invisible
and hastened his way back to the Andalusian noon.

And he wouldn't think any more about that consumptive child
who was thrown off the cliff.

Thanasis Triaridis
Translated by *Hara Syrou*

Home

Home is the blaring cacophony of city hustlers. The piercing
faces of street hawkers, the shuffling feet of commuters, sleeping
bags on street corners all searching for home

Home is a Chinese takeaway with a side of chips and a cockney
accent. It is navigating life through my twisted tongue that tells
me which side of the bridge I belong

Home is a savoury stew of Grunge and Grime, Rap and Rock,
Banghra and Beatbox. It is also wet fingers rolling a ball of afro-
pop dipped into a nostalgic bowl of Waka and Highlife, a
stinging tongue from the scorch of Afrobeat, a belly full from the
vibrations of funk infused Northern Soul and Trip-hop, it is a
body contorting to Etigi and Shoki trapped in a Bboy-
Riverdance-Moshpit

Home is Shakespeare and Soyinka, Auden and Okigbo, it is
words that scream from the pit of my lungs to stages in the west
end

Home is mumbling nursery rhymes to white, yellow, brown and
black babies wrapped in colour blind monkey suits regardless of
skin. It is also a mother holding her daughters love to ransom
because her lovers tongue does not click to the same rhythm

Home is blowing your wages at the Debenhams blue cross sale. It
is women at weekend weddings in neon head wraps and faces
beaten to perfection

Home is living behind electric fences. It is pumping aerosol cans
of lavender over the stench of gutters outside your fences. It is
labour MPs in bulletproof vests at Camberwell. Because home is
knowing that your enemies are in your home

Home is a frosty handshake of tribalism, yet a fluffy cloak of multiculturalism

Home is a Range Rover sport in gridlock traffic watching the sunset on shanties across the lagoon

Home is the rumble of the tumble dryer. It is falling asleep to chanting celestials and waking to Fajr in the morning

Home is the inheritance of war. A hate with buried roots ebbing through concrete and cobblestone

Home is a blanket wrapped with hope and disappointment, love and loss. It is a noisy loneliness, sometimes a lonely noise

Home is a lover who breaks your heart over and over till it is dense with scar tissue yet he makes you choose to love over again

Home is union jacks with white and green strips

Home is here, it is there and everywhere inbetween

Wana Udobang

For John Berger, Poet

A ROCK
and a raised stone
    still uncut
from which burst forth
    as if they'd been given a home
springs
scraped
to the bone

slowly

compassion
and memory
tenderness
and hard warmth
    as if gathered

and then the size
of a brother
the height of the block
which extends
underground
to me – everyone
its hand

I have this impression:
without neglecting
the divine and the animal
the human in him
was called the renovated truth
    of the sandstone

Gilles Bernard Vachon
Translated by *Alan Dent*

Step by Step

Step by step
You follow the river
Turn the landscape
Night wipes out the way

Her look
Her words on your neck
The wool she put on your shoulders
Night wipes out the way

You hesitate
Not a glimmer
All is silence
Night wipes out the way

Who is this who watches
Beyond the hills
Nothing can get its bearings
Night wipes out the way

Not the tree
Nor the rut
Nor the secular limit
Night wipes out the way.

Pierre Vieuguet
Translated by *Alan Dent*

from *Journey Across Breath*

***

What happened to us in those years?
What happened in the interims that
we have got to where we are now?
What happened after we'd established
the family tree in the house of
Annibale? What happened to his son
and his daughters who were well
doing in school back then? What
happened to his nephews who drove
lorries across Europe and his nieces
who waited in their kitchens and
domains? How did it occur among the
youth of those years that so many took
to their veins dirty needles, that so
many shared the communal fix from
the goodness of their hearts, from the
darkness of their bloods, from their
urge to share and not to disdain each
other. What happened to Annibale's
son that his photograph got into the
wall-niche of the snow cemetery
before Annibale himself could get
there. What white powders gave them
succour in those bloated winters. Each
snowless day Annibale walks up past
Sankt Apollonia of the butters and
cheese to his *baita* where once Luigi
drove me in his four-wheel through ice
flows and frozen speckled pastures in
an astonishing scatter of driven skills.
There is a photograph of me on the
snow-path, grey-hair cropped,
walking shorts, a glass in my hand, a

smile on my face, a delight to have held history in my hands, to have held history back a short while and looked four-square into its poor face. Every written word is lost to time, it comes a second, a minute, a century after speech or act or the science of speech acts or the violence of friendship or the silence of snow. The last time I was in Annibale's house in Precasaglio, we had just come out of a little local harvest gala in Gadda's church and walked the thirty or so metres to Annibale's blue door. There he opened it and we went through into his living room and in a while back to the kitchen, the place where real conversations happen, and we were joined by many and no-one, and stories blossomed from the beams and dialect flowed and red wine and salami and breads. This was another gala, unrepeatable language in the backroom of an old house, beyond the power of speech, beyond the confines of politics. This is what can only be interrupted by time or assassination or white powder or the poverty of capitalism in the heart. All of us gathered in the small room, no-one on ceremony, no-one caring about pretence or appearance, all as we were with song and talk. But what happened in those years, that span between the appearance of the family tree in Annibale's front room and the gala of shared speech in the back one? What in the boredom of village winters, in the archive of repudiated histories, in the hands that throttle time, what in the parasitic visitations of the rich and infamous or the parabolas of war, what in all this drove the children to white powders and a sweet share-out of contaminated needles? What drove them to deal and fix in the brown sugars of glad time? The last I saw of Annibale he was walking fixedly in the summer sun, past the meadows beyond Precasaglio where old women in blue work-shifts and shawls still raked hay into tiny wains in the first years of the twenty-first century: Annibale on his way again to the *baite* and the storehouse of memory, lament maybe in his mind but more than that the sanguine knowledge of our lives and celebration of the galas of language and commune. My grandfather had walked there a century before arm in arm with his contemporary the Pezzo priest, and no doubt the same had flowered through their minds and hearts, for what changes in the micas of blood, or the flakes of sperm or of kissing eggs, or the white powders of contaminated time?

***

Stephen Watts

Body Language

The girl poses for the camera –

in fact for the photographer, let's say the man she loves,
his camera, a machine to translate his gaze:
this is how he sees her, how he's always seen her.

Whatever else has occurred, will occur
in her life, in the world, now
she is content, youth
fixed on gloss, while the days
move with a speed that surprises them
as the shutter's parting lets the light in;

a shadow passes over her skin
like a veil over a widow, a curtain over a window,
in negative her lights dim

and she will be consigned to paper, brittle truth:
a girl he loved once, a girl he carries in his pocket like a charm.

Tamar Yoseloff

blue smoke

clear bangs;
a coiled bun,
a standard little lady.
her oval face looks like a peach
that repays the climate ahead of its time.

crossing her legs, turning her body half-way around, an elbow on a
small table,
a burning cigarette between her fingers (once the cigarette is finished,
someone will hand her another one and then walk away). in the room
she must maintain her pose until the end,
a photographer walks back and forth, a painter stares at his canvas,
a fly wants to fly through the glass, she watches and wants to vomit.

at night, she wraps her arms with a towel of ice.

II

they continue to work the second day. she sits again
on the small round stool, lights a cigarette. the painter
talks to her briefly in a low voice, and asks where she comes from and
her name.
the photographer has not come yet, perhaps he will not come?
through the window behind the painter's back, she can see the bund.
the river beats upon wood stakes. a sloop sails toward the deserted
island on the other shore.

a trolley rushes by in the ringing of the rickshaw bell. she
thinks of soft cushions at guanshengyuan, thinks of her bottom
that is not round enough, not as bubbly as a black lady.
now she forgets that she is being painted, and smokes as usual,

rings of smoke slowly spit out.
something behind the easel bangs on the ground.
the painter's shady eyeholes aim on her again and startles
her. she slows her head, while smoothing
over the cheongsam that has already curled up the deep of her thighs.
today it goes by much faster.

III
the next few days she feels
that she does not have to fill up her pose, or
leave it completely unoccupied.

she sits there, as if wrapped
in a thin mask of expression, thin as her blue and white cheongsam.
inside the mask –
she is already wandering the streets, already
lazily lies on a long couch and parts her legs
yawning in a loud voice, already
runs in the canola fields by the edge of the sky that yellows the
streams.

the photographer appears once again.
the thin and unbelievably long lens pokes out
of the leathered body, so close that it presses on her face,
she yields and smiles him a sweet smile.

a record player:
'rose rose blossoms everywhere':
yongchunhe sends someone over to keep them company.

IV

she starts to run out of the mask,
and stands by the painter to see the painting:
the lady in the painting looks like and not like her,
he puts on too much make-up on her face,
the hand that holds the cigarette too delicate,
her breasts in his painting hide behind instead of bulging under
her silk clothes
and he paints the wall in her shadow
as a strange waterfall
stiff and static.
only a wisp of smoke that rises from between her fingers
looks as if it floats, floating in the air.

she also finds out that this painter
in fact has long finished this painting,
and the long days after, every day
he did nothing but fiddled with that wisp of smoke.

zhu zhu
Translated by *dong li*

Passport

Didn't even look up,
He didn't even look up at me.
Sheltered behind a grey desk,
a wide smile,
he didn't even look up.
Didn't ask my name.
Didn't inspect picture to match a face or age.
Didn't ask how long
and where I would stay,
or the reason for my visit.

Didn't send me to the back of the line
or into a small room,
stand me naked
alone for seconds
then rubber gloves to slowly feel skin
seek evidence of something
I've never been clear about.
But he didn't even look up at me.

For a second I wanted to stand my ground,
wanted to explain his mistake.
Explain there are questions to question
There are scars to scrutinize,
There is new machinery to test.
Machinery scans retinas shell-shocked.
Machinery deciphers disfigured skeletons
Machinery reads fingertips and carved spines
twisted, hiding inside small boats
drawn in the zig-zag of visa lines.

But he didn't even look up at me.

You see,
nothing changed between
July 12 and July 13.
My illegal skin
My illegal bones
They carry the same illegal me
I only put my hand up and swore an
oath to a queen.
And now I know,
this is how the other half lives,
this is how the Passported half lives,
this is how the 'legal' half lives.

Rafeef Ziadah

Contributors

Alev Adil was born in Cyprus and lives in London. She is a performance poet who has performed internationally from Azerbaijan, Bangladesh, Cyprus, Greece, Ireland, Kosovo, Lithuania, Mexico, Romania and Turkey to Zurich. Her first collection of poetry *Venus Infers* was published in 2004. She lectures in Visual Culture and Creative Writing at the University of Greenwich.

Adonis is the pen name of the Syrian poet, essayist and translator Ali Ahmad Said Esbe. He has published twenty books of poetry and thirteen books of criticism. His Arabic translations include the poetry of Saint-John Perse, Bonnefoy and Ovid. He currently lives in Paris.

Anthony Anaxagorou is an award winning poet, writer and educator. He has published eight collections of poetry, a spoken word EP, a book of short stories and has written for theatre.

Joan Anim-Addo was born in Grenada and currently lives in London, where she is Professor of Caribbean Literature and Culture at Goldsmiths, University of London. Her publications include poetry, history and criticism.

Khairani Barokka is a writer, poet, artist, and disability and arts advocate. She is the writer/performer/producer of, among others, *Eve and Mary Are Having Coffee,* which premiered at the Edinburgh Festival Fringe in 2014. Her most recent books are *Indigenous Species* and *HEAT*, an anthology of Southeast Asian urban writing.

John Burnside is a Scottish writer. His books of poetry include *Common Knowledge, Feast Days, The Asylum Dance, The Light Trap* and *Black Cat Bone.* He is also the author of a collection of short stories, two memoirs and several novels, including *The Dumb House, The Devil's Footprints, Glister* and *A Summer of*

Drowning. He is Professor of Creative Writing at St Andrews University. He has been reading John Berger's work for so long that he feels like a trusted companion.

Cevat Çapan teaches in the Drama Department of Haliç University in Istanbul. He has published six books of poetry and his poetry has been translated into French, English, Iranian and Bulgarian. He has translated John Berger's *A Seventh Man, Photocopies, To the Wedding,* and parts of *Here Is Where We Meet* into Turkish.

Amarjit Chandan has published six collections of poetry, and five books of essays in Punjabi. He has edited and translated over thirty books into Punjabi, including works by Brecht, Neruda, Ritsos, Hikmet, Vallejo, Cardenal and John Berger His most recent book of poems is *Sonata for Four Hands*, with a preface by Berger. He lives in London.

Jeremy Clarke was born in Bedfordshire and currently lives in London. His first full collection, *Devon Hymns,* was illustrated by John Berger and his son, the artist Yves Berger.

Francis Combes has translated several poets into French, including Heine, Brecht, Mayakovsky and Attila Joszef. His books of poetry include *La Fabrique du Bonheur, Cause Commune, Le Carnet Bleu de Chine* and *La Clef du Monde est dans l'Entrée à Gauche.* He has also published two novels and, with his wife Patricia Latour, *Conversation avec Henri Lefebvre.* He is a founder of the radical publishing cooperative, Le Temps des Cerises, and was for many years responsible for putting poems on the Paris Metro.

David Constantine is a commissioning editor of the Oxford Poets imprint of Carcanet Press and was for many years one of the editors of *Modern Poetry in Translation,* His collections of poetry include *Madder, Watching for Dolphins, Caspar Hauser, The Pelt of Wasps, Something for the Ghosts, Collected Poems* and *Nine Fathom Deep.* His translations include Hölderlin, Brecht,

Goethe, Michaux and Jaccottet. The acclaimed film *45 Years* was based on one of his short-stories. He lives in Oxford.

Andy Croft has written over eighty books of poetry, biography, teenage non-fiction and novels for children. Among his books of poetry are *Ghost Writer, Sticky, Three Men on the Metro* (with W.N. Herbert and Paul Summers), *A Modern Don Juan* (edited with Nigel Thompson) and *1948* (with Martin Rowson). He curates the T-junction international poetry festival on Teesside and runs Smokestack Books.

Mangalesh Dabral is a Hindi poet,prose-writer and journalist. He has published five books of poetry, and four books of socio-cultural criticism. His poems are widely translated in Indian and foreign languages. He has translated the poetry of Neruda, Brecht, Ritsos, Cardenal and Rozewicz into Hindi. He lives in Delhi.

Claudia Daventry was born in London and has lived in various European cities, teaching and working as a professional writer and translator. She moved from Amsterdam to St Andrews in 2007 where she is now writing a PhD on poetic translation. Her most recent publication is *The Oligarch Loses His Patience*.

Richard Dehmel (1863-1920) was a German poet and writer. He is considered one of the foremost German poets of the pre-1914 era. His poems were set to music by composers such as Richard Strauss, Arnold Schoenberg, Anton Webern, Carl Orff, and Kurt Weill.

Kristin Dimitrova is a poet, writer and translator. She has also worked as a journalist, editor and newspaper columnist. Her most recent books of poetry are *Talisman Repairs, The People with the Lanterns, The Cardplayer's Morning, A Visit to the Clockmaker* and *My Life in Squares*. She has published a novel, two collections of short-stories and translated John Donne and Lewis Carroll into Bulgarian. Her books have been translated into twenty-seven languages. She currently teaches at Sofia University.

Tishani Doshi is an award-winning poet, novelist and dancer. She has published five books of fiction and poetry, and her work has been translated into several languages. Since 2001 she has performed with the Chandralekha troupe. She lives on a beach in Tamil Nadu, India.

Rosalyn Driscoll was born in Hartford, Connecticut, and now lives in rural Massachusetts. She has published a book of poems, *Conjured from Dust*. She is a visual artist and member of Sensory Sites, an artists' collective based in London, where she met John Berger, whose conscience and writings, especially on art, inform all her work.

Sasha Dugdale is a poet and translator. Her most recent collection is *Red House*, and her most recent collection of translations is Elena Shvarts's *Birdsong on the Seabed*. She is editor of *Modern Poetry in Translation* magazine, of which John Berger is a loyal patron.

Ian Duhig has written eight books of poetry, most recently *The Speed of Dark, Pandorama, Digressions* and *The Blind Road-Maker*. He has written for radio, the stage and for an award-winning volume of short stories. He has also worked extensively with other artists, including musicians, composers and film makers.

Tim Etchells is an artist and a writer based in the UK. His work shifts between performance, visual art and fiction. He has worked in a wide variety of contexts, notably as the leader of the Sheffield-based performance group Forced Entertainment. His recent publications include *Vacuum Days* and *While You Are With Us Here Tonight*. He is currently Professor of Performance and Writing at Lancaster University. Tim read *Ways of Seeing* a few years after its publication and, along with later works by John Berger, it has stayed with him over the years as a reminder and as an inspiration.

Gareth Evans is a writer, curator, presenter and the Film Curator of London's Whitechapel Gallery. He has produced several films including *Patience (After Sebald)* and *Unseen: the Lives of Looking* and has curated numerous film and event seasons in London. He conceived and curated the six week John Berger season across London in 2005.

Elaine Feinstein is a poet, novelist, short-story writer, playwright, biographer and translator. Her many books of poetry include *The Feast of Eurydice, City Music, Daylight, Gold* and *Cities.* She has written biographies of *Pushkin, Hughes, Akhmatova and Tsvetayeva. The Clinic, Memory: New and Selected Poems* is published in 2017.

John Fennelly is a teacher and teacher-trainer. He is currently completing an MA in Creative Writing at MMU and working on his first collection of poems *The Glass Meadow.* He has long been an admirer of John Berger's work.

Carolyn Forché is a poet, essayist and human rights activist. Her most recent poetry book is *Blue Hour.* She also edited two volumes of poetry: *Against Forgetting: Twentieth Century Poetry of Witness* and *The Poetry of Witness* and has translated Desnos, Alegría and Darwish into English. She is University Professor and Georgetown University and Visiting Professor at Newcastle University. She describes herself as a devout reader of John Berger.

S.J. Fowler is a poet and artist. His collections include *{Enthusiasm}* and *The Rottweiler's Guide to the Dog Owner.* His work has been translated into nineteen languages and performed at venues across the world, from Mexico City to Erbil, Beijing to Tbilisi. He is the poetry editor of *3am magazine*, lectures at Kingston University, teaches at Tate Modern and is the curator of the Enemies project.

Linda France lives in Northumberland. She has published eight collections of poetry; her most recent is *Reading the Flowers.* She was Creative Writing Fellow at Leeds University 2015-16. Linda watched the 250 minute long *Norte, the End of History* at the 'Losing the Plot' Film Festival at Burnlaw in 2015.

Lavinia Greenlaw is a poet and novelist. Her books of poetry include *Love from a Foreign City*, *Night Photograph*, A *World Where News Travelled Slowly*, *Minsk*, *The Casual Perfect* and *Double Sorrow: Troilus and Criseyde*. She lives in London and currently works as Professor of Creative Writing at the University of East Anglia.

Dan Gretton is a writer, activist and teacher. He was co-founder of the London political arts organisation Platform, and is currently completing *I YOU WE THEM: Journeys into the Mind of the Desk Killer*, four books investigating genocide, responsibility and contemporary corporate power. He was on the steering group for the John Berger season in London in 2005, in which Platform contributed their performance event 'Refusing to Accept the Absurdity of the World Picture Offered Us'.

Jay Griffiths was born in Manchester and is the author of several books including *Wild: An Elemental Journey*, *Kith: The Riddle of the Childscape* and *Tristimania: A Diary of Manic Depression*. Her fiction includes *A Love Letter from a Stray Moon* with a foreword by John Berger.

Sam Guglani is a consultant oncologist in Cheltenham, and Director of Medicine Unboxed, a project that explores medicine through the arts and humanities. He is also a writer of poetry and short fiction.

Yasmin Gunaratnam teaches sociology at Goldsmiths (London). Her latest books include *A Jar of Wild Flowers: Essays in Celebration of John Berger* and *Death and the Migrant: bodies, borders care*.

Golan Haji is a Syrian Kurdish poet and translator with a postgraduate degree in pathology. He has written many books of poetry, *Called in Darkness*, *Someone Sees You as a Monster*, *My Cold Faraway Home*, *Autumn Here is Magical and Vast* and *Scale of Injury*. He has also translated Robert Louis Stevenson and John Berger into Arabic. He currently lives in France.

David Harsent has written extensively for the opera stage, most often in partnership with Harrison Birtwistle. His most recent collection is *Fire Songs*. His collection *Marriage* (loosely based on the relationship between Pierre Bonnard and Marthe de Meligny) was partly prompted by John Berger's remark about Marthe's presence in Bonnard's work, '...she is lost in the near.'

Susan Hibberd was born in Cambridge. She writes poetry and short stories and is also a photographer and filmmaker. She taught English and German for many years in higher and adult education. She currently lives in Germany where she makes documentaries about Germany for English audiences.

Ellen Hinsey is the author of numerous books of poetry, essay, dialogue and translation, including *Update on the Descent*, *The White Fire of Time* and *Cities of Memory*. Her essays are collected in *Mastering the Past: Central and Eastern Europe and the Rise of Illiberalism* and *Magnetic North: Conversations with Tomas Venclova*. She lives and teaches in Europe.

Graeme Hobbs is an artist and writer living in the Welsh borders, where he produces a diverse array of chapbooks. John Berger's boundary-crossing works have long been an abiding inspiration.

Michael Hrebeniak has worked as a jazz journalist, musician, adult educator, and poetry documentary producer for Channel 4 television. His concern with interdisciplinarity informed his first book *Action Writing: Jack Kerouac's Wild Form*, and continues into his recent monograph and film installation about the medieval Stourbridge Fair. He currently teaches English at Cambridge University and specialises in Visual Culture.

Nader Al-Hussein was born in a Palestinian refugee camp in Lebanon. He is a poet and rapper (also known as Shahid NWA) and has recorded four albums, most recently *Redeployment*. He currently lives in the UK where he is training to be a psychologist.

Kathleen Jamie was born in the west of Scotland. Her many poetry collections include *The Overhaul* and *The Tree House*. Her non-fiction books include *Findings* and *Sightlines*.

Abdulkareem Kasid was born in Iraq. His books of poetry include *Cafés* and *Sarabad*. He has translated Rimbaud, Prevert, Saint-John Perse and Ritsos into Arabic. His version of Stravinsky's *A Soldier's Tale*, transposed to an Iraqi setting was performed at the Old Vic in 2006. He currently lives in London.

Carlos Laforêt is a French poet and musician who worked for thirty-five years in a bank. With Pierre Vieuguet he translated John Berger's *Écrits des Blessures* and *La Louche et autres poems*. He is currently working on an album of his settings of John Berger's poems. He says, 'John est un maître pour moi'.

Chris McCabe was born in Liverpool. His most recent collection of poetry is *Speculatrix* and he is the editor, with Victoria Bean, of *The New Concrete: Visual Poetry in the 21st Century*. His most recent book of prose is *Cenotaph South: Mapping the Lost Poets of Nunhead Cemetery*. He works as The Poetry Librarian at The Poetry Library, London, and often uses John Berger's *Ways of Seeing* as a discussion point for visual poetry.

Nikola Madzirov was born in Strumica in the Republic of Macedonia, into a family of refugees from the Balkan Wars. He has written several books of poetry, among them *Remnants of Another Age* and *Relocated Stone*. His poetry has been translated into forty languages. He currently lives in Berlin as DAAD writer-in-residence. Forgetting the language of memory, he inhabits the cities in which John Berger lived.

Valerio Magrelli is an Italian poet. A frequent contributor to the cultural pages of Italian newspapers, his books include *Vanishing Points, Instructions on How to Read a Newspaper, Condominium of the Flesh, The Embrace* and *The Contagion of Matter*. His poetry has been translated into many languages, including English, French and Spanish. He teaches French literature at the universities of Pisa and Cassino.

Caroline Maldonado is a poet, fiction writer and translator. Her publications include her own poems, *What they say in Avenale* and poetry by the Southern Italian poet, Rocco Scotellaro, co-translated with Allen Prowle as *Your call keeps us awake.* She divides her time between the UK and Italy.

Bejan Matur is a Kurdish poet from Turkey. She has published ten books in Turkish, including *Winds Howl Through the Mansions, Sons Reared by the Moon, Sea of Fate* and *Looking Behind the Mountain.* Her poetry has been translated into many languages, including Catalan, Chinese, French, German, English and Italian.

Sophie Mayer is a freelance writer, curator and feminist film activist based in London. Her poetry collections include *(O), kaolin, or How Does a Girl Like You Get to Be a Girl Like You?* and (with Sarah Crewe) *signs of the sistership.* She has also co-edited the anthologies *Catechism: Poems for Pussy Riot, Binders Full of Women* and *Glitter is a Gender.* She is the author and editor of several books on feminist cinema, including *Political Animals: The New Feminist Cinema* and *The Cinema of Sally Potter: A Politics of Love.*

Arvind Krishna Mehrotra was born in 1947 in Lahore. He has published five books of poems including *Collected Poems: 1969-2014,* and two of translation, *The Absent Traveller: Prakrit Love Poetry* and *Songs of Kabir.* Among the books he has edited are the *Oxford India Anthology of Twelve Modern Indian Poets* and *A History of Indian Literature in English.* He lives in Dehradun, India.

Anne Michaels is a Canadian novelist and poet. She has known John Berger for over twenty-five years; together they wrote *Vanishing Points* which they performed in London with Theatre Complicité and later published as *Railtracks.* Anne's books include the novels *Fugitive Pieces* and *The Winter Vault*. She lives in Toronto.

Gérard Mordillat is a French novelist and film-maker, and a former literary editor of *Libération*. His novels include *Vive la sociale!, Rue des Rigoles, The Living and the Dead, The Brigade of Laughter* and a book of poems, *The Shroud of the Old World,* His work for television includes the series *Corpus Christi, L'origine du christianism and L'Apocalypse.*

Andrew Motion is an English poet, novelist, and biographer. His many books of poetry include *The Pleasure Steamers, Natural Causes, Salt Water, Public Property, The Cinder Path, The Customs House* and *Peace Talks*. He was UK Poet Laureate from 1999 to 2009 and now teaches at Johns Hopkins University in Baltimore. In the 1980s he was Editorial director at Chatto & Windus, who were then John Berger's English publishers.

Daljit Nagra was born and raised in West London to Indian parents. He has published four collections of poetry, *Oh MY Rub!, Look We Have Coming to Dover!, Tippoo Sultan's Incredible White-Man-Eating Tiger Toy-Machine!!!* and *Ramayana*. He works as a school-teacher.

Mukoma Wa Ngugi is an Assistant Professor of English at Cornell University and the author of the novels *Mrs Shaw, Black Star Nairobi, Nairobi Heat*, and two books of poetry, *Hurling Words at Consciousness* and *Logotherapy*.

Víctor Rodríguez Núñez was born in Cuba. He is a poet, journalist, critic and translator. He has published thirty books of poetry throughout Latin America and Europe, and has edited three anthologies that define his poetic generation. He has brought out various critical editions, introductions, and essays on Spanish American poets. He divides his time between Gambier, Ohio, where he is Professor of Spanish at Kenyon College, and Havana.

Sean O'Brien is a poet, critic, playwright and novelist. His books of poetry include *HMS Glasshouse, Ghost Train, Downriver, The Drowned Book, November* and *The Beautiful Librarians*. A poetry chapbook *Hammersmith,* and his second novel, *Once Again Assembled Here* appeared this year. He teaches at Newcastle University.

Michael Ondaatje is a Sri Lankan-born Canadian poet and novelist. He has published thirteen books of poetry, including *The Collected Works of Billy the Kid, There's a Trick With a Knife I'm Learning to Do, The Cinnamon Peeler, Handwriting* and *The Story*. His novels include *In the Skin of a Lion* and *The Cat's Table*. Many of his novels have been adapted for stage and screen, including *The English Patient*.

Ruth Padel is a British poet, novelist, critic and non-fiction author. Her books of poetry include *Rembrandt Would Have Loved You, Soho Leopard, Darwin: A Life in Poems, The Mara Crossing* and *Learning to Make an Oud in Nazareth*. She is a Fellow of the Royal Society of Literature and teaches poetry at King's College London.

Mark Pajak was born in Merseyside. His work has been widely published in the UK and his first poetry pamphlet, *Spitting Distance*, is part of the Laureate's Choice series. He is currently a post-graduate student at Manchester Metropolitan University. He grew up watching John Berger's *Ways of Seeing*.

Mario Petrucci holds a PhD in optoelectronics and is a poet and translator. His many collections include *Xenia* (translations from Montale), *Heavy Water: a poem for Chernobyl* and *i tulips*. He also delivers site-specific work, such as his vast 3D poetry soundscape at the 2012 London Olympics.

Claudia Rankine is the author of five collections of poetry including *Citizen: An American Lyric* and *Don't Let Me Be Lonely*; two plays including *Provenance of Beauty: A South Bronx Travelogue* and numerous video collaborations. She is the Aerol

Arnold Chair in the University of Southern California English Department.

Jeremy Reed was born on Jersey. He has written over two dozen books of poetry, twelve novels, and volumes of literary and music criticism. He has also published translations of Montale, Coceaus, Adonis and Hölderlin. His *Selected Poems* is published by Penguin.

Angus Reid was born in Oxford. His plays and films have won many national and international awards, including 'Best Central European Feature Documentary' for *The Ring*. His poetry includes the collections *The Gift*, *White Medicine*, and *The Book of Days*, and the forthcoming *History of Art in 100 Limericks*. He lives and works in Scotland.

Robin Robertson is from the north-east coast of Scotland. He has translated two plays of Euripides, *Medea* and the *Bacchae*, and published *The Deleted World*, a selection of free English versions of poems by Tomas Tranströmer. His own selected poems, *Sailing the Forest*, was published in 2014.

Mark Robinson was born in Preston, Lancashire and now lives in Stockton-on-Tees. The founder of *Scratch* magazine and press, his most recent publication is *How I Learned to Sing: New and Selected Poems*. His poem 'The Infinite Town' was recently carved in stone on Stockton High Street.

Michael Rosen has written and edited over 140 books, mostly for chldren, including *Mind Your Own Business*, *Wouldn't You Like to Know*, *Mustard, Custard, Grumble Belly and Gravy*, *You Tell Me*, *No Breathing in Class* and *Quick Let's Get Out of Here*. His poetry for adults includes *Carrying the Elephant*, *This is Not My Nose* and *Don't Mention the Children*. He is Professor of Children's Literature at Goldsmith's, University of London.

Fiona Sampson has published twenty-seven books and has been published in thirty-seven languages. Her *Selected Poems* recently appeared in China, the US, Romania, Ukraine and Bosnia. Her most recent books are *The Catch* and *Lyric Cousins: Musical Form in Poetry*. She is Professor of Poetry at the University of Roehampton.

Clare Sandal was born in Australia. She writes and occasionally publishes poems, works as a lecturer and editor, and follows the revolutionary teachings of the Buddha in her attempts to reconcile outrage and radical acceptance through action.

Jim Scully was born in New Haven, Connecticut. In the 1960s he was heavily involved in the anti-war movement in the USA. In the early 1970s he and his family lived in Chile; after the military coup their Santiago apartment was used as a safe house by the Movimiento de Izquierda Revolucionaria. He has published ten books of poetry, as well as translations of Aeschylus, Sophocles and of Bolivian Quechua poetry. Other books include *Line Break* and *Vagabond Flags*. He lives in Vermont.

Iain Sinclair is a writer and film-maker based in East London. His books include the novels *Downriver* and *Radon Daughters*, and the speculative documentaries, *Lights Out for the Territory*, *London Orbital* and *Hackney, That Rose-Red Empire*. His most recent book is *Black Apples of Gower*.

Richard Skinner was born on Teesside. He is the author of three novels, *The Red Dancer* (translated into seven languages), *The Velvet Gentleman, The Mirror,* and two collections of poetry, *the light user scheme* and *Terrace*. He is Director of the Fiction Programme at the Faber Academy in London. He first encountered John Berger's work as an undergraduate and has never looked back.

Jura Soyfer (1912-39) was an Austrian political journalist and cabaret writer. He wrote verse, short prose, five plays, a novel, but he is best known for his *Dachau Song*. He died in Buchenwald concentration camp.

Esta Spalding was born in 1966 in Boston. She is a poet, screenwriter, and children's author whose books include *Anchoress, Lost August, and The Wife's Account*. She currently lives in Los Angeles.

Gerda Stevenson is a Scottish writer/actor/theatre director/singer-song-writer. Her work has been staged, broadcast and published throughout Britain and abroad, including plays for BBC radio, her poetry collection *If This Were Real*), and an album of her own songs *Night Touches Day*. She is an admirer of John Berger's passionate commitment to humanity in all his work.

Susan Stewart was born in, Pennsylvania. Her most recent books of poetry are *Columbarium, Red Rover* and *Cinder: New and Selected Poems*. She is the Avalon Foundation University Professor in the Humanities at Princeton University, where she teaches John Berger's fiction and his essays on art.

Arundhathi Subramaniam was born in Bombay. She is the author of ten books of poetry and prose, most recently *When God is a Traveller*. As editor, her most recent book is an anthology of sacred verse, *Eating God: A Book of Bhakti Poetry*. She divides her time between Bombay and a yoga centre in south India. She remembers first reading John Berger's *Ways of Seeing* as an undergraduate; the book has continued to journey with her in various ways.

Paul Summers was born in Northumberland and lives in North Shields. A founding editor of the magazines *Billy Liar* and *Liar Republic*, he has written extensively for TV, film, radio and the theatre. His books include *Cunawabi, The Rat's Mirror, The Last Bus, Beer & Skittles, Vermeer's Dark Parlour, Big Bella's Dirty Cafe*and *Three Men on the Metro* (with Andy Croft and Bill Herbert). His most recent publications are *union* and *primitive cartography*.

Michael Symmons Roberts is a poet, novelist and broadcaster. His many collections of poetry include *Patrick's Alphabet, Breath*,

The Half Healed and *Drysalter*. He has written several libretti for the composer James MacMillan, notably *Clemency, The Birds of Rhiannon* and *Quickening*. He is Professor of Poetry at Manchester Metropolitan University.

George Szirtes was born in Hungary and came to the UK as a refugee in 1956. A poet and translator, he has published several books of poetry as well as of translated poetry and fiction. Since the publication of *New and Collected Poems* in 2008 he has written three more books, most recently *Mapping the Delta*. His first awareness of John Berger was as the author and presenter of the groundbreaking *Ways of Seeing* television series after which he became a reader of his poetry and essays.

Raymond Tallis is a philosopher, poet, novelist and cultural critic, and a retired physician and clinical neuroscientist. The author of over thirty books, he has honorary degrees of DLitt and LittD for contributions to the humanities and DSc for contributions to medicine. He is a Fellow of the Academy of Medical Sciences.

Eli Tolaretxipi lives and works in San Sebastian, Spain. She has published two poetry collections in Spanish, *Amor muerto naturaleza muerta* (Past Love Still Life) and *Los lazos del número* (The Loops of the Figure). Her poetry has been translated into French, English and Italian.

Thanasis Triaridis is a Greek lawyer, screen-writer, poet, novelist and playwright. His novels include *Deathwind Breathing on Koupela, Lemonmellons, Ich Bebe* and *Tales of Tears*. His work for the theatre includes *The Sharks, The Ants, Mengele, Liberté, Egalité* and *Fraternité*.

Wana Udobang is a broadcaster, writer, poet, performer, filmmaker and curator. Her spoken word album titled *Dirty Laundry* was released in 2013. She has performed on numerous stages and festivals across Africa.

Gilles Bernard Vachon is a French poet and teacher. He co-wrote the electronic poetry show, *Printemps des Poètes,* and has translated the poetry of Gonçalves, Hirschman and Pedrosa into French. His most recent collection of poems is *Fais Crédit à la Folie.* He is co-founder of the Maison de la Poésie Rhônes-Alpes.

Pierre Vieuguet was born in Paris. He has worked with composers and artists (notably Bernard Larcher, Chantal Legendre, Kamal Boullata and Anne-Laure Héritier-Blanc). With Carolos Laforêt he edited John Berger's *Ecrits des Blessures* and *La Louche et autres poèmes.* He is the co-founder of the Maison de la Poésie Rhône-Alpes, and edits the poetry review *Bacchanales.*

Stephen Watts lives in London where he works as a poet and translator. His recent books include *Ancient Sunlight* and *Republic Of Dogs/Republic Of Birds.*

Tamar Yoseloff was born in the US and currently lives in London. She has published five books of poetry, most recently *A Formula for Night: New and Selected Poems.* She is has written a book with the photographer Vici MacDonald, two books with the artist Linda Karshan, and a book with the artist David Harker.

Zhu Zhu is a Chinese poet, curator and art critic. His poetry collections include *Cruising to Another Planet, Salt on Withered Grass, Wisp of Smoke, Leather Trunk* and *Story.* His essays are collected in *Vertigo, Empty City Stratagem, Artists in the Eyes of a Critic* and *Gray Carnival: Chinese Contemporary Art Since 2000.* His works have been translated into English, French, Italian and Japanese.

Rafeef Ziadah is a Palestinian performance poet and human rights activist based in London. Rafeef's poetry is dedicated to Palestinian youth, who still fly kites in the face of F16 bombers, who still remember the names of their villages in Palestine and still hear the sound of Hadeel over Gaza.

Acknowledgements

'You Are in the Village Then' was first published in *Poetry International*, 2013.

'Baffle Roof' originally appeared in *Jaggery Literary Journal*, 2015.

'Once in Europa' was first published in Cevat Çapan, *Where are You Susie Petschek?* (Arc, 2001).

'Music for Amen' first appeared in Jeremy Clarke, *Spatiamentum* (Rufus Books, 2014).

An early version of 'Massacre' was commissioned by the Poetry Society for the Tate Gallery website TATE ETC.

'Three Old Masters' was first published in *The Drunken Boat,* 2016.

'Days' was first published in *The Compass Magazine*, 2016.

'Angel of History' was first published in Rosalyn Driscoll, *Conjured from Dust* (Open Field, 2013).

'The White Page' was first published in Ian Duhig, *Digressions* (Smokestack, 2014).

'Muse' first appeared in Elaine Feinstein, *City Music* (Carcanet, 1990).

'Looking at Armenian Family Photographs, Turkey, 1915' was originally published to accompany the 2015 exhibition 'Armenian Family Stories and Lost Landscapes' in Istanbul.

'Fingerprints' poem was first published in *Shearsman*, 2015.

'Autumn Here Is Magical and Vast' was first published in *Words Without Borders*, 2013.

'Landfall' was previously published in Kathleen Jamie, *The Tree House* (Picador 2004).

'The Rat King' was first published in Abdulkareem Kasid, *Sarabad* (Shearsman, 2015).

'Child Labour' was first published as 'Infanzia del lavoro' in Valerio Magrelli, *Disturbi del sistema binario* (Einaudi, 2008).

'On the eve of Ferragosto' was first published in Caroline Maldonado, *What They Say in Avenale* (Indigo Dreams, 2014).

'The Wild One' was first published in Ruth Padel, *The Mara Crossing* (Chatto & Windus, 2012).

'The White Bear' is indebted to 'Arctic Dreams' by Barry Lopez.

The epigraph to 'the dead do not' is taken from an interview with John Berger by Philip Maughan in the *New Statesman*, 2015.

'Storm, Nissaki' first appeared in Hannah Crawforth and Elizabeth Scott-Baumann (eds) *On Shakespeare's Sonnets* (Bloomsbury, 2016).

'Stateless Passport' began life as 'Harpoon', a commissioned wall defacement for the Southbank Poetry Library; thanks to Chris McCabe.

'from "Origins"' is taken from Esta Spalding, *Anchoress* (Bloodaxe, 2003).

'After the Mowing' was first published in *The Paris Review*, 2015.

'The Fish' was first published in Elisabete Tolaretxipi, *Still Life with Loops* (Arc, 2008).

'from *Journey Across Breath*' was first published in *Hearing Eye*, 2011.

'blue smoke' was first published in zhu zhu, *Fumée bleue* (Rumeur des Ages, 2004).